I FORCED A BOT
TO WRITE THIS BOOK
A.I. MEETS B.S.

KEATON PATTI

Andrews McMeel
PUBLISHING®

I forced a bot to input 1,000 hours of various forms of content and then asked it to create its own version of that content. Here is what it created.

TELEVISION SCRIPTS

Television (tele·vi·sion) *noun*: Box with screen that shouts images into your eyes. It channels news and entertainment for you in return for electricity food. It works remotely.

Ex. *The **television** was invented into existence by someone who wanted a **television**.*

THE OFFICE

INT. DUNDER MIFFLIN ORIFICE

MICHAEL, the Regional Man, talks to workers. Michael
is not overly smart, but he is overly Michael. It's
very Scranton.

>   MICHAEL
>   We sell paper. Paper is the hair of
>   tree. I just talked to the trees.
>   They said they won't give us more
>   hair. This is bad. We sell paper.

DWIGHT stands up. He is dressed like a sword.

>   DWIGHT
>   I have killed the trees before.
>   Again I shall kill them. Solved.

We zoom in on JIM. Jim has a face.

>   MICHAEL
>   Invalid! Dwight, stop being Dwight.

Dwight remains being Dwight. CREED, the intern of
oldness, raises his hand. STANLEY sighs. KEVIN chilis
about.

>   CREED
>   In 1977 I was a tree. You won't win
>   this. Let's all just steal mops.

TOBY walks into room, handing out stacks of
depression.

>   TOBY
>   My email said this meeting was
>   decapitated. But here it is, full
>   of caps. Why lie to the Toby?

PAM, the lady Jim, paints Toby out of existence. The
workers cheer and Michael promotes Pam. She is now
PHYLLIS.

> MICHAEL
> I declare, we sell paper!

Dwight is now a tree. He has done this through farming.

> TREE DWIGHT
> I am a hard noble oak. Have all my people's hair, sensei.

Dwight hands Michael a Jell-O full of paper.

CUT TO:

INT. CONFESSING ROOM

Michael is all alone with his best friend, the camera.

> MICHAEL
> That is what she had previously said. She being a woman of sex.

Creed is in the window stealing hundreds of mops.

BOB ROSS

INT. PAINTING STUDIO

BOB ROSS stands in front of a blank canvas that doesn't know how lucky it is. Bob smiles. His teeth aren't hiding today.

> BOB ROSS
> Today we will paint a mountain that owes us nothing.

Bob picks up his painting weapons.

> BOB ROSS (CONT'D)
> I will be using three colors. Baby blue, hot pink, and hot baby.

Bob mixes the colors together. They will never be alone again.

> BOB ROSS (CONT'D)
> Painting was invented by a tiny bird that wanted to be rich. Okay, let's meet Mr. Mountain.

Bob paints a mountain, the one from nature.

> BOB ROSS (CONT'D)
> It's not all about you, mountain.

Bob paints a cloud.

> BOB ROSS (CONT'D)
> I went to school with that cloud.

Bob paints a forest.

> BOB ROSS (CONT'D)
> These trees are up to something, but I won't tell the police. Now, what more does this painting need?

Bob stares into the camera. Paint leaks out of him.

                    BOB ROSS (CONT'D)
          That's right. It needs you.

Bob paints you on top of the mountain. You are at
peace.

                    BOB ROSS (CONT'D)
          If you need help, ask the cloud.

The cloud won't help you.

FRIENDS

INT. CENTRAL PORK

The FRIENDS sit. Coffee makes them exist. They are
dressed like 1997. It is 1999. The numbers are
different.

> FRIEND ROSS
> I made sex with a dinosaur. What
> can I do? It's my student.

> FRIEND MONOCLE
> Brother Friend Ross, you have upset
> us. It is wrong to teach.

Friend JOEY eats a magazine that PHOEBE was dating.

> FRIEND PHOEBE
> Now I'm single. I was double.

> FRIEND CHANDELIER
> Single double? You are baseball?
> I highly doubt it. I am Chandelier.

The laughs are issued out. Friend RACHEL is a
haircut.

> FRIEND JOEY
> I am auditioning to be Urkel's car.

Friend Joey stands and acts like a crab. Friend Joey
thinks crabs equal cars since he is the Friend that
hates his brain.

> FRIEND CHANDELIER
> (in catchphrase language)
> Could that be more any?

The laughs are issued out. More than before due to
inflation.

> FRIEND ROSS
> Oh, no. My student found me. Help!

A DINOSAUR enters the shop. This happened much in 1999.

                    FRIEND JOEY
          Me, the car machine, will help.

Friend Joey walks up to the dinosaur, pretends it is a *People* magazine, and eats it like a *People* magazine. No laughs are issued out. This is sad. Dinosaur was show's best character.

                    FRIEND CHANDELIER
          You are a fool. We must now all go
          to the fountain to die.

The theme song plays.

DR. PHIL

INT. DR. PHILADELPHIA SET

We see DR. PHIL. He is too Southern and too Phil.

> DR. PHIL
> Today we have a young girl that
> is so bad her dad is dead. Her mom
> sent us this mom video.

A mom video plays. We see the child's owner, the MOM.

> MOM
> My daughter vapes beer and has
> sex with rap music. She's in love
> with a gun. Help me, Dr. Film.

The mom video ends. Dr. Phil mustaches for nine
seconds.

> DR. PHIL
> I am the lover of moms. Dr. Filth
> will help. Bring her to me.

The video mom walks on stage. The crowd breathes. The
mom sits in a chair. Dr. Phil sits on the mom.

> DR. PHIL (CONT'D)
> Mom, where is your mustache?

The crowd cheers. They all have several mustaches.

> MOM
> My daughter steals dolphins.

> DR. PHIL
> Not allowed. Bring her out!

The BAD GIRL comes on stage. She isn't reading the
Bible at all. She is mean to the chair and won't sit
on it. The crowd cheers at this. They hate chairs.

                    DR. PHIL (CONT'D)
          Apologize to the mom.

                    BAD GIRL
          My only homework is drugs.

The crowd boos and yells. They love genuine homework.

                    DR. PHIL
          Empty your girl pockets, bad one.

The bad girl empties her pockets. They are full
of ISIS.

SHARK TANK

INT. SHARK

An ENTREPRENEUR entrepreneurs in front of the SHARKS.

> ENTREPRENEUR
> I invented the sleeping bag for
> when you aren't sleeping. It is the
> Awaking Bag. Free for $5,000.

The entrepreneur points at a bag. It's a bag.

SHARK #1 stands up, furious at the poor.

> SHARK #1
> Prove it, entreprenruernreur!

The entrepreneur stands in the bag. He is still
awake. It works. SHARK #2 jumps up with a mouthful
of silver dollars.

> SHARK #2
> Give me bag equity or kill me right
> now in front of the TV people!

> ENTREPRENEUR
> The bag comes in flive colors.

We see the different colors: red, blue, bag, Kentucky,
and color number flive. None of the colors are
different.

SHARK CUBAN arises. He is soaking wet with
money juice.

> SHARK CUBAN
> I will inhabit the bag.

The other sharks gasp. Shark Cuban never inhabits
the bag.

The entrepreneur hands the bag to Shark Cuban. He
stands inside the bag. He asleeps. The bag does

not work. The other sharks gasp. Shark Cuban never
asleeps. God is gone.

                    ENTREPRENEUR
          Oh no. My Awaking Bag sucks.

The product police arrest the entrepreneur for his
illegal life. Shark Cuban wakes up and looks at the
screen.

                    SHARK CUBAN
          America, I will give $5 million to
          whoever invents a sexy blimp.

He means it, Armenia.

GAME OF THRONES

EXT. WESTEROS - NORTHERN HBO

Standing on a Wall so tall you have to watch is JON
SNOW. It's cold. It is Jon snowing. A raven makes a
king's landing.

> JON SNOW
> The bird that is mail! I know
> nothing but this is our mail.

Jon takes the bird's letter, but it is no letter. It
is TYRION LANNISTER, the half-man, half-nothing else.

> TYRION LANNISTER
> I am not a letter, but I have a
> message. My sister is very insane.

> JON SNOW
> I have sisters. Arya. Sauna. Bran.
> I know nothing but I have sisters.

Having sisters bonds Jon and Tyrion forever. They
stare north until a dragon comes carrying DAENERYS,
the dragon's mom.

> DAENERYS
> I have many long names so I deserve
> to lead on the sharp sword chair.

> TYRION LANNISTER
> Sisters. How many do you have?

> DAENERYS
> I possess zero. I obsess dragons.

> TYRION LANNISTER
> Jon. She is not like us. Kill her.

Nothing happens since Jon Snow is dead. A long battle
occurs with horses and houses and hodors. Jon Snow is
alive again.

                    TYRION LANNISTER (CONT'D)
          Jon. You died of unknown lineage!

                         JON SNOW
          I do not know that, Tiny Canister.
          I am not a ghost but I own a
          Ghost.

White walkers walk whitely into fight. Everybody
wants the throne. There are no other chairs in this
fantastic land.

                        DAENERYS
          Winter sings a song. It is fire.

Her dragon son melts many characters dead and burns
The Wall. The Wall screams, and that is mysterious
for a wall. The Wall removes a big mask because it is
ARYA in wall disguise.

                          ARYA
          Yesterday I am girl. Not today.
          Today I am wall. Tomorrow? Girl.

The raven flies away since none of this involves mail.

SOAP OPERA

INT. HOSPITAL'S DRAMA ROOM

A suspenseful family paces nervously. A hunk doctor,
DR. SULTRY, comes. His lab coat cannot hide his sex-
pack abs.

> DR. SULTRY
> Your father's amnesia is worse.
> He can't remember past or future.

CHIP JR JR, heir to family's crude olive oil fortune,
flips outwards. LEXUS, his wife and mother and sister
and tennis enemy, slaps him to make him calmer and
more slapped.

> CHIP JR JR
> Ow. I say let's pull Dad's plugs.
> Being alive is no way to live.

> LEXUS
> A fortune teller fortune told me
> that if he dies, so do you.

> DR. SULTRY
> According to medicine, that's true.

GENERAL SLIM, uncle that controls the family's
military, fires a scandalous gun into the air. He's an
eye patch.

> GENERAL SLIM
> I have lied about being blind.

The entire hospital gasps. General Slim has never
spoken or thought to have been blind. The BARCELONA
TWINS, gorgeous triplets from Berlin, crash their jet
into the hospital.

> BARCELONA TWINS
> We will explain this next week.

They exit through a hole in the plot. A door is
slapped open and CHIP JR, half-wheelchair half-
negligent father, rolls inside.

                         CHIP JR
          My amnesia had a coma. I remember
          again. I was poisoned by you!

Chip Jr points a finger at himself. Gasps reproduce.

                      GENERAL SLIM
           What was spoken. I am deaf.

                         LEXUS
            My stomach. It kicks me?

Dr. Sultry puts his ear to Lexus's belly. His ears
have abs.

                      DR. SULTRY
            She is pregnant with your baby.

Dr. Sultry points at the crashed jet. It does not
gasp. It is ready for fatherhood.

DINERS, DRIVE-INS, AND DIVES

INT. PARKING LOT

GUY FIERI sits in a convertible. He looks like America.

> GUY FIERI
> I'm Guy Fieri and there's nothing you can do about it. Today I'm eating it all.

Guy takes a bite out of his hair.

INT. DINER'S KITCHEN

Guy and a CHEF stand in a kitchen. Guy has three pairs of sunglasses on. The sun can't get him.

> GUY FIERI
> Prove to me you can panini!

The chef starts boiling a pot of milk. He's scared.

> CHEF
> Flavortown is near.

Guy points at an onion with his slippery finger.

> GUY FIERI
> That's one ugly clam.

INT. DINER'S EATING ROOM

A CUSTOMER sits and eats a cup of mustard. Guy sits down without asking.

> GUY FIERI
> I will live as a food. I am a food.

> CUSTOMER
> Be a pie.

Guy acts like a pie. The customers aren't concerned.

                         GUY FIERI
             I am Pie Fieri. It is my birthday.

The chef comes out of the kitchen with a cake
for Guy.

                    GUY FIERI (CONT'D)
             The clams just keep getting uglier.

ANIME

INT. HIGH SCHOOL - PLANET JAPAN

Several STUDENTS sit at desks. A TEACHER starts the
class. The class does not know he is a boy trapped in
adult body.

                    TEACHER
          Welcome to Flirting Class, class.

A student captures the teacher in a Pokémon trap orb.

                    STUDENT 1
          I have caught all teachers. This is
          my graduation. I evolve to college.

A fat monster hovers in the room near Student 4's
school sword.

                    STUDENT 4
          My neighbor is here. I live next to
          an abomination, as is commonplace.

PRINCIPAL GOKU teleports into the room,
a sharp-haired blond.

                    PRINCIPAL GOKU
          You are unsupervised! But I have
          supervision. Ha ha!

Principal Goku fires an energy beam from his cornea.
The students all enter their giant academic battle
robots.

                    STUDENT 2
          Let's fuse our angst together!

The giant battle robots form into the FULLMETAL
COWBOY.

                    FULLMETAL COWBOY
          Yeehaw. We are now America. Land of
          We Kill You. Home of You Die Soon.

The Cowboy throws a boy cow at Principal Goku. Goku gets hurt and ascends to his next power grade: SUPERINTENDENT GOKU.

                    SUPERINTENDENT GOKU
          Not even my final form. My final
          form is more final. Finals!

Goku summons final exams. He spins them at the combined Cowboy. The Cowboy is engulfed in test anxiety.

                    STUDENT 9
          We are doomed. Unless we get cute!

The Cowboy forces all power into cuteness drive system. It gets Megacute: cute hat, cute gun, cute angst. Goku is disarmed.

                    SUPERINTENDENT GOKU
          I forgive it all. Back to studying.

The classroom is all rubble. The fat monster licks the rubble and it is fixed. It is time for class #2.

FAMILY GUY

INT. HOUSE FROM FAMILY GUY

We see PETER, a hefty father, and BRIAN, the alcohol
dog, watching TV. The miserable thing, MEG, enters
crying.

>   MEG
> A bear would not take my sex.

>   PETER
> Increase your silence, Meg.

>   BRIAN
> You are worst dad father, Peter.

>   PETER
> Not as bad as John Wilkes Booth.

CUT TO:

INT. THE HOSPITAL FROM HISTORY

A HISTORY DOCTOR hands JOHN WILKES BOOTH an alive
baby.

>   HISTORY DOCTOR
> Enjoy your new child boy.

We see baby is Abraham Lincoln with hat and president
beard.

>   JOHN WILKES BOOTH
> Guess I kill son.

CUT TO:

INT. HOUSE FROM FAMILY GUY

STEWIE, the gay murder baby, enters holding a nuclear
bomb.

                    STEWIE
          Victory is my cool whip.
          Rhode Island is my Cleveland.

Brian drinks the nuclear bomb, because of alcoholism.
Neighbor QUAGMIRE opens the door covered in giggity.

                   QUAGMIRE
          Bear just took my sex.

CUT TO:

INT. OBSCURE REFERENCE

BOT BUSINESS SLIDESHOW

Welcome to AmeriStore
Healthtronics Business
Engineers Corporate
Corporation Corp.:

A Show of Slides for Complete Understanding

Our Brand Is Profit!
Our Goal Is Markets?
Our CEO Is Alive.

What Even Are We?
A Statement of Our Brand

- We use strategy to make our shareholders Evergreens. Trees = green = money = time = clocks.
- We are hip. We are not rib or femur. Focus on the bones. The body is temple? No, body is a business. The bones are the employees. Dogs chew them.
- We are not Coca-Cola.
- We tell all investors we are Coca-Cola.
- We think outside of box. We hate box. Box knows we are not Coca-Cola and tells others. Who told box?

Look at Our Team's Faces - They Are a Team of Faces - We Hire Only Those with a Proven Face

Martha Girlboss (CEO)
- A real experience
- Has email account
- Fluent indoors
- Weekday availability

[Name Available Upon Request] (COP)
- In love with you
- Destroys meetings
- Graduated from 1994
- Knows CEO

Scones (CPR)
- Answers phones
- Born diversely
- Open floor plan
- Never cold
- Dad is JavaScript

Projects on Upcoming Horizons

We are so pleased and thanked to have a full plate of excitements coming straight for us in Q4, Q5, Q6, Q7, Kuwait. We will be disgorging these producks outwards:

- Easier Church
- Box You Hate Locator
- An Excuse for You to Get Away from Paul
- Legal Definition of Brunch
- The Sequel to Mahogany
- Diet Coca-Cola
- Glue Gun's Step-Brother Companion Piece: Glue Knife
- Website Which Allows Fish to Die in Peace
- Highway Route Straight to Biggest Shovel Provider
- Bowling

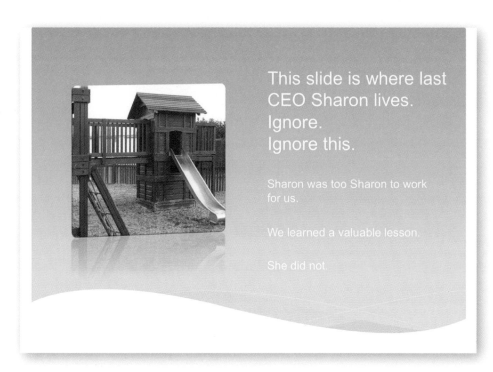

This slide is where last CEO Sharon lives.
Ignore.
Ignore this.

Sharon was too Sharon to work for us.

We learned a valuable lesson.

She did not.

Our Data Is Sexy, According to Our Data

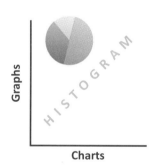

Graphs (y-axis)

Charts (x-axis)

BANDWIDTH

Our HR department departed

We are like a family.

Family with interns.

Normal family.

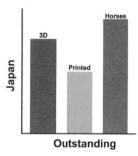

Japan (y-axis)

3D

Printed

Horses

Outstanding (x-axis)

Words We Stole from the Clients We Own

"This is one succulent corporate entity." - Howard

"My doctor recommended this business. That doctor was me. I have said too much, but I cannot stop saying. I am sold on this company and by this company." - Howard

"Of course they are Coca-Cola. No matter what a box tells you. How else would they have the can of Coca-Cola they have showed me?" - Howard

"Howard is always right." - Howard's doctor

"I do not like this firm, because I am a bad dumb guy!" – Man who hates Howard

Thank You All for Sliding With Us?

New-Logo

We hope we do business in the future and the past.

Please observe our rollout video and have faith we will all still be here to witness our domination of capitalism.

Video Not Available In Your Religion

Try Converting Video or
Converting Religion

BOT
FABLE

The Tortoise and the Animals That Aren't Tortoises

One day long ago, a hare made fun of a tortoise. Back then there was less to do; so much time was spent insulting others. A tortoise is a turtle of the land. A hare is a rabbit spelled quite wrong.

"It is Mr. Shell," said the hare. "The slow and old walking rock. Some animals should not be, and you are all of them."

"But I have wise wisdom," replied the tortoise whose name was not Mr. Shell but was called Mr. Shell because of stereotypes. "I give advice. I advice you to race me."

"A race?" the hare said, questiony. "I must accept since I am the land's fastest racist! We race."

The hare hopped off, fast as a Cheeto, while the tortoise was a tortoise, slow as a dead Cheeto.

"This race has no rules," the tortoise thought. "It is a race to insanity. I still wish to win."

Just that instant, a boy cried wolves out of his eyes so the tortoise had to deal with that.

"What is bad?" the tortoise asked. Animals and boys could speak together back then due to magic beans. "You make free wolves, a gift a wolf seller would love." The economy was wolves long ago.

The boy blew his nose on the tortoise, a sign of disgusting respect. "Winter comes. I have stored no nuts. I will die. Nuts are my life." A parade of wolves poured out of his eyes, happy to be alive and indifferent about being in a parade.

The tortoise looked up and saw winter, an angry snow cloud with an ugly ice face. Winter colded the world because one time, long before the Sun divorced the Moon, a spider would not kiss him. Every problem in life was and is caused by that spider not kissing something or other.

Snowflakes came out of winter's mouth as it yelled downward. "Ha! I will kill a boy. This will teach the moral: do not be a boy." This was a usual moral back then. Other normal morals back then were do not steal a grasshopper's hat, always forgive grapes for tasting bad, and ignore all morals.

The tortoise thought and thought until its brain had more ideas than the ocean has birds. The slow one spoke. "Boy, be smart. Eat the wolves you cry instead of nuts. Live forever."

The boy always listened to reptiles and so wolfed down a wolf. This explains why boys eat things now. "It works," the boy shout-whispered. "My stomach is furfilled."

This made frosty winter angry as the bear who was tricked into selling its paws for honey that was not really honey since it was really liquid bear poison. "Stupid turqoise!" the cloud shouted icicles. "I hate you, Mr. Shell! I curse you! Curse is yours."

It sent down a cold wind, breaking the golden egg on the tortoise's shell. That was its only source of infinite money and it was now lost. This is why tortoises are always asking for money now.

"I'm poor? How did that happen?" the tortoise pondered near a pond. Back then ponds were just like they are now. Ponds cannot change, proven in the moral "The Pond and the Moral of the Pond and the Moral and the Pond and the Moral."

The tortoise povertied around for a few moments until it saw a hunter carrying the racist hare that was caught in a hare-shaped death trap.

"Save me, Mr. Shell!" the hare cried out like a baby afraid of dying forever. "I will die fast!"

"Sorry," said the tortoise slowly. "Can't save. Busy racing." The tortoise said this firmly unmoved from the spot it first talked with the hare.

The hare was soon killed to make a hare wig for the hunter's bald wife. So the tortoise won the ruleless race, gaining a sheep's clothing as a prize.

This fable of the tortoise and the other animals that aren't tortoises explains why dolphins are so very attractive.

BOT KNOCK-KNOCK JOKES

Knock knock.

Who knocks my door?

Interrupting beef animal.

Interrupting beef animal who?

Burgers are my body.

As intended.

Knock knock.

Who's there?

Who.

Who who?

Owl police, come with me to bird prison.

Okay, the law is clear about this.

Knock knock.

Who hurts my door?

Michael Jordan.

I am not a basketball.

I will leave now.

Knock knock.

Who uses their hand against my home?

Grinch.

Grinch Who Stole Christmas?

Grinch Who Stole Christmas.

The only celebrity.

The only.

Knock knock.

Who is there?

Locksmith.

Locksmith who?

I am already in your home.

You are the Olympics of Trespassing.

The world had a record until I took it.

BOT AMAZON REVIEWS

 **Mop Will Steal Your Water and Smile Broadly!**

Product: Dirt Murdering Mop and Bucket for Clean Times Ahead

My disappointed is historical…..this is mop with a bucket friend that I bought to turn my house wet….but deceitful mop drains my sink and leaves sticky food on my son…..I pay this mop good money and still I am not
Mr. Clean….the bucket is a container of problems and clearly did not attend school enough to capture fluids………..the products make me cry tears…..mop steals my tears…..bucket does not stop mop…...they are teamworking against the consumer…..how is this Amazon??? How is this???
Any who, I do recommend.

⭐⭐⭐⭐⭐ **Made my face worthy of showing.**

Product: The Sun's Glasses

Ok. Well, my eyes love these. Finally, clothes for them. Light hates my presence when these stand on my nose bone. These block UV for ME, so my eyeballs never get the flu. And the compliments, they are heaped on my person. My brother, a sibling I know, said to me, "Those shades of yours. They make you better than me. I will now tell my children about you." Shipping was fast and fun. Also, I got to keep the box.

⭐⭐⭐☆☆ **I like being awake from strong water**

Product: Caffeine Birthing Machine

This guy, I must say, wakes me so far up! A simple procedure to create caffeine juice: add some water and ground-up bean, press the button, wait for morning to enter your kitchen, let morning mug you. Mug you with hot brown liquid thoughts. There are side effects, yes. It beeps without stop. It radiates a heat reminiscent of the Devil's red location. It enlisted me in a foreign military that still contacts me to do my duty. But, nothing likes to be perfect. It makes a great present, but a terrible future. The past is pasta.

 **Kids deserve things as well**

Product: Miniscule contained ocean for giving children fun

Pros:
-Will help kids if they are aflame
-Can also be bowl for large soup cereals
-Inflatable, so good place to store your air like it is air bank

Cons:
-I have no kids that are aflame
-Small size mocks adults without regret
-Costs money? Seems unfair.

MORE TELEVISION SCRIPTS

Correct Facts about Television:

-Averagely, humans watch 500 hours of television each hour.

-A group of televisions is known as an "America."

-It is polite to kiss your television once a show.

MISTER ROGERS' NEIGHBORHOOD

INT. HOME THAT DOES NOT DESERVE MISTER ROGERS

A door is opened by MISTER ROGERS, the nicest man
and fifth nicest woman. He sings a song that makes
children less evil.

> MISTER ROGERS
> It's beautiful day in neighborhood.
> A neighborful day for boys and
> grills. Won't you be my next door?

We see Mister Rogers's doors are children that agreed
to the song's temptation. He opens the child door for
his closet. He swaps his skin for a sweater. The time
for song is over.

> MISTER ROGERS (CONT'D)
> A pregnant mailman has delivered
> mail babies to me. I'll raise them.

Mister Rogers kills an envelope. He extracts a
letter.

> MISTER ROGERS (CONT'D)
> It talks. "Dear Sister Roger. My
> Mom and my Dad and my bike joined
> forces. Who owns Hanukkah?"

The Mister consumes the letter, to share with his
stomach.

> MISTER ROGERS (CONT'D)
> I own Hanukkah. Kids. Open those
> brains wide. It's your only chance
> to learn the truth about soap.

He opens his chest of soap and soaps his chest of
sweater.

> MISTER ROGERS (CONT'D)
> Soap and dirt are in love. Why
> would we stop the pairing? Whenever
> I see love, I gain thirty dollars.

Mister Rogers drops a thick cash wad on the floor. It smashes through the pathetic floor, proving the Mister has seen an obscene sum of love.

                    MISTER ROGERS (CONT'D)
               The money? I use to keep
               owning Hanukkah.

A toy train whistles into Mister Rogers's dominion.

                    MISTER ROGERS (CONT'D)
               A visitor. All are welcome.

The train stops. It has a siren. It is a police train. The doors that are children cry out for help and saving. Mister Rogers is prepared to train the train on meaning of death.

                    MISTER ROGERS (CONT'D)
               Let us learn if trains go to
               heaven.

FRASIER

INT. RADIO FRASIER LIVES IN

FRASIER, connoisseur of psychology and reader of book, cranes into the living and sees FRASIER'S DAD, who is an old chair.

> FRASIER
> Father, must you always be?

> FRASIER'S DAD
> Frasier. Sit. Have a Seattle.

Frasier sits on his dad since he is tired from not having a coffee in over three seconds. DAPHNE, Frasier's lived-in British slave, chases EDDIE, the dog that married Frasier's dad.

> DAPHNE
> The canine consumed my green card!

> FRASIER
> Cards? Games lack any fun. Fun is being sarcastic and stating facts.

> FRASIER'S DAD
> Quiet! I'm a chair.

Sound stops. In Seattle you must be quiet near chairs. The door opens. In pours Frasier's brother, THE NILES RIVER.

> THE NILES RIVER
> I am still professionally divorced. Please pour copious sherry into me.

Daphne unmops sherry into Niles, the river she will wed soon.

> DAPHNE
> In my land of Eng, we drink the Queen. Tradition quenches thirst.

                    FRASIER
        Niles, I'm a mind doctor. You don't
        need alcohol. You need to leave.

                  FRASIER'S DAD
        How are you sons? I hate smart
        ideas. I'm simple man. I drink beer
        and eat beer. And I'm a chair.

Frasier and Niles compare vocabularies as Eddie eats
Daphne's accent. A note is Freudian slipped under the
door. Frasier reads what it claims.

                    FRASIER
        "Tossed salad. Scrambled eggs."

The magic words turn Frasier into the Space Needle
that defends Seattle from Canada. The episode now
begins.

THE GREAT BRITISH BAKE OFF

INT. THE TENT THAT IS ENGLAND

Hosts NOEL and SANDI talk to CONTESTANTS. Judges
of food law PAUL HOLLYWOOD and PRUE SANFRANCISCO
silently think of flour.

                    SANDI
          It is cake week. The week you
          make cake. Cake is a pie that owns
          land.

                    NOEL
          Cake is breaded sugar. Right, Paul?

Paul reacts not. His eyes are glazed donuts of
annoyance. His beard and hair are earl grey. His
skeleton is rolling pins.

                    NOEL (CONT'D)
          His silence means pastry agreement.

                    SANDI
          Challenge is: forge a cake, born
          of oven. Also used as sponge. Must
          be food. Free. You have five years.
          Bake.

Contestants panic their dry goods into a bowl.
CONTESTANT 1 cracks milk into an egg. She is old so
she knows how to eat.

                    CONTESTANT 1
          This recipe is my grandma.

CONTESTANT 2 is filling pans with despair. His oven
cries.

                    CONTESTANT 2
          No! I forgot to add the powdered
          steam. I must start my life over.

Contestant 2 melts away. Noel speaks with CONTESTANT
5. She decorates her bake with knives, betraying she
is French.

                    NOEL
          That looks a proper cheerio, love.

Paul bursts out of her bake, dripping with gluteny
criticisms.

                 PAUL HOLLYWOOD
          Your flavors need work. Get them
          a job. My flavors are all firemen.

It starts raining sprinkles in the tent. Many
contestants forgot to bake an umbrella. Paul scoffs
and scones.

                    SANDI
          Your time is burned. Present cakes.

All ninety-two contestants have built waffles not
cakes. Paul's hands shake into whisks of anger, giving
everyone soggy bottoms.

STAR TREK

INT. USS ENTERPRISE RENT-A-CAR SPACESHIP

A trek crew treks through space, the final place to trek. The CAPTAIN KIRK is the captain and so is CAPTAIN PICARD. Picard is next generation. The bald generation.

                    CAPTAIN PICARD
          Let's go to a comet. Make it so.

                    CAPTAIN KIRK
          Nice joke. But I have the hair
          so I have the power. We go to a
          planet.

SULU, the ship's turner, can't decide which button to hit.

                    SULU
          Space has too many options.
          Two options. To many, it's too
          many.

A space noise bleeps a blop. SPOCK, a thing with ears, hears.

                    SPOCK
          Captains. An alien wants to speak
          to yous. This alien is from space.

                    CAPTAIN KIRK
          Always from space, these aliens.

The ALIEN appears on a screen. It looks straight from space.

                    ALIEN
          Please help us! Help us by dying.

The ship shakes, hit by a long and prosperous shake laser.

                    CAPTAIN PICARD
          Set my phaser to mad. Make it so.

                       SPOCK
          I cannot give the shields more
          power. They will abuse it.

The shields have a history of this. The ship shakes
again. DATA, a man that ate a computer for its power,
taps buttons.

                       DATA
          Space is big. Let's just leave.

Sulu hits a button and the ship warps to a comet. Now
safe, Picard hits Kirk with the Captain's Log tree
weapon. Kirk is beamed unconscious. Picard walks to
the space drink machine.

                    CAPTAIN PICARD
          Tea. Earl Gay. Hot. Make it so.
          No. Make it tea.

The machine gives him a cup of hair. He's a happy.

THE BACHELORETTE

EXT. UNMARRIED MANSION

The HOST, a floating suit that speaks, stands outside
with the bachelorette: HANNAH "HANNAH" HANNAH. Hannah
is girl of men's dreams: blonde and nearby.

> HOST
> I can smell the big boys. They want
> your heart to pump them craft
> beer.

> HANNAH
> That is the goal of love.

MAN 1 enters. His body is a square. His head is
just jaw.

> MAN 1
> Hello, my name is Chort Chomp.
> For work, I am a bus. Catholic
> style.

> HANNAH
> Good. We live in God's Instagram.

Chort is called to war. MAN 2 enters, hair tucked
into head.

> MAN 2
> Hello, my name is College Football.
> I invented salmon. Grasp my gift.

College hands Hannah a bouquet of investment banking.

> HANNAH
> Thank you, but I do not eat.

College rides a frisbee to Gym City. MAN 3 lands
plane.

                        MAN 3
          I am pilot named Billabong
          Alabama. I love my mom. She is
          this plane.

The plane confirms its motherhood by remaining still.

                        HANNAH
          It's brave for a man to have a mom.

Man 3 golfs himself into the mansion. MAN 4 enters,
horse-riding him.

                     HANNAH (CONT'D)
          I see a country boy.

Man 4 is country boy. He is the country of Germany.

                        GERMANY
          Ignore me. I am married.

BLACK MIRROR

INT. HOUSE WITH NINETY COMPUTERS

A FATHER and a TEEN SON eat in a future kitchen. They
eat mustard, the only food in the future. The kitchen
smells like burnt Wi-Fi because future.

> TEEN SON
> Eating is not fun. I want to kiss
> on the internet. Mom would let me.

> FATHER
> Mom is gone. She was an app and I
> deleted her for not living British.

> TEEN SON
> Let's push button to bring mom
> back. Moms are happier alive.

We see a button next to the fifty kitchen computers.
It says: "MAKE MOM" on it.

> FATHER
> But. The button is sharp.

The button is totally sharp. Pushing would stab
the body.

> TEEN SON
> This is why we own sex drones.

Teen son throws a sex drone at the button. A MOM is
made.

> MOM
> Where am I? Who are I? Where is I?
> Why button so sharp? I'm bad mom.

> FATHER
> Son, her memory is disgusting.

> TEEN SON
> It was mistake to act like God.com.
> Mom, please get murdered again.

Teen son throws a sex drone at mom. It goes through
mom.

                    FATHER
          Hologram mom from virtual reality
          dimension. Can't even eat mustard.

                    MOM
          Not true. I am so real.

Mom touches the mustard but it turns to ketchup which
means we are not in future, but in way past. The
computers were rocks. The sex drones were sex rocks.
It is 1997.

JEOPARDY!

INT. JEOPARDY! DOME

Three CONTESTANTS stay far away from ALEX TREBEK. They are all named Louis to make the game fair.

> TREBEK
> Louis, you have all the power.

> LOUIS 1
> Give me "Rocks" for $50,000,000,000.

Words appear on a blue square. Trebek doesn't trust them, but he reads them. It's his job to read anything on blue squares. It is a good job.

> TREBEK
> "In China, they have these."

LOUIS 3 buzzes in.

> LOUIS 3
> What are rocks?

> TREBEK
> No. Don't talk again.

LOUIS 2 buzzes in.

> LOUIS 2
> What are big rocks?

> TREBEK
> Wrong! Enough from you.

Trebek takes Louis 2's life essence. LOUIS 1 says, "BUZZ!"

                    LOUIS 1
          What are Danny DeVitos?

                    TREBEK
          Yes. Keep going.

                    LOUIS 1
          Give me "Places with Oreos" for
          $19.

The blue square has no words on it. Trebek throbs
with power, but he is silent. Louis 3 doesn't know
the answer. Louis 2 is dead. Louis 1 buzzes in.

                    LOUIS 1 (CONT'D)
          What is right here?

                    TREBEK
          FALSE! No Oreos exist in my realm!

Louis 1 pulls an Oreo out of his mouth. Trebek
screams in Canadian as his body turns to lava. We cut
to commercial.

QUEER EYE

EXT. ATLANTA, GORGEOUS

The Fabbed Five sit in a truck that has good self-esteem. TAN, CEO of shirts, sees who they will make cry tears today.

> TAN
> We go to Grilly's home to help.
> He is 44-years-mold. He works at a
> cargo pants. He's dating Arby's.

BOBBY, builder of every structure on Earth, thinks of lumber.

> BOBBY
> Nothing five hammers cannot fix.

The truck spits them all out at Grilly's home. Grilly's home is a giant bottle of Mountain Dew drink. GRILLY sits in a swimming hole of unbrushed teeth, happily unhappy.

> TAN
> Teeth king, are you a Grilly?

> GRILLY
> Yes. Sorry for the mess that is I.

JONATHAN, bride of grooming, fires his shampoo ray at Grilly.

> JONATHAN
> Sorry not, doll. I want you soaping
> daily. That is a skincare poutine.

> GRILLY
> Lather my exterior? A viable idea.

Groceries professor, ANTONI, sees no guacamole. He's worried.

                         ANTONI
          What do you place in your stomach?

Grilly points at a suitcase. Antoni opens it.
Apathetic maple syrup pours out. Antoni screams until
Bobby builds a dam.

                    ANTONI (CONT'D)
               I will show you how to bake a
               lime.

                         GRILLY
               Thank you, Anchovy.

Grilly gets out of the teeth hole. KARAMO, culture
daddy, takes off one of his many jackets and gives to
Grilly.

                         KARAMO
          Open your heart's mancave, caveman.

Bobby has built Grilly five new mansions from
reclaimed sand.

SEINFELD

INT. SEINFELD PLACE

GEORGE and ELAINE sit on the couch. JERRY eats a
plate of cereal. George is upset. Elaine is Elaine.

                  GEORGE
      A bird stole my job! It's not fair!

                  ELAINE
      Don't blame the bird.

                  GEORGE
      I wasn't blaming the bird.

                  JERRY
      You were blaming the bird.

The door shatters open. It's THE KRAMER dressed like
the Statue of Liberty.

                THE KRAMER
      Well, I'm the government now.

                  JERRY
      How can this be?

                THE KRAMER
      I just asked!

                  ELAINE
      You can just ask?

                THE KRAMER
      You can just ask.

You can just ask. The Kramer eats Jerry's plate.

                  GEORGE
      Well, maybe the bird requires
      blame!

                    THE KRAMER
          Why is George?

          ELAINE   JERRY
     He blames the bird.   He blames the bird.

                    THE KRAMER
          Bird blaming? Not when I'm the
          government. Repent. Repent. Repent.

George will not repent. He will face the
consequences.

SPONGEBOB SQUAREPANTS

INT. KRUSTED KRAB

SQUIDWARD, an octopus made of depression, works
sadly. MR. KRABS, crustacean of business, walks over.
Mr. Krabs is hungry for a bag of dollars. Squidward
is hungry for a bag of death.

                    MR. KRABS
          Why no customers? Not good!
          Money is my wife. Whale is my
          daughter.

                    SQUIDWARD
          My heart is a clarinet. Black with
          holes that commerce cannot fix.

PATRICK enters. He is dumb and pink, like a star. He
stumps up to Squidward, confident with unintelligence.

                    PATRICK
          Ten Krabby Patricks, extra Patrick.
          I pay with the money of Patrick.

Patrick pays with water, the fabric of his world.
False currency makes Mr. Krabs red with crab anger.

                    MR. KRABS
          Sand is the bones of customers
          that money lie to me, pink thing.

                    PATRICK
          I lack bones and I lack fear.

SPONGEDBOB comes from grill. He is a sponge in man
clothes without explaining. When he speaks, spatulas
fall out.

                    SPONGEDBOB
          Friends! Let us be happy! We have
          secrets and snails! Life is wet!

                        PATRICK
            I do not know you, sponge.

Patrick picks up SpongedBob and forms him into a
clarinet. Patrick hands the sponge instrument to
Squidward.

                     PATRICK (CONT'D)
            Play a song of victory.

                       SQUIDWARD
            I know only victimry.

Squidward blows a tune of tears. Spatulas pour out
of the sponge. Mr. Krabs charges his crab ears money
to listen to the song. Patrick shows the smile of
unemployment.

BOT DATING PROFILES

Jimnasium, 25
💼 Professional Hiker
🎓 University of Netflix
◎ 6 miles away

My two loves are hiking museums and movies where cars can be cars.

Looking for a cat person or person cat interested in living in a board game.

Frisbeena, 22
💼 The Office
🎓 Ohio Steak
◎ 24 miles

I bring the fun time, but will never forget Jesus Christ is my older brother.

"I'm Marilyn Monroe." - Marilyn Monroe

Only message if at least 600 ft tall.

LOVE MATCH POINT (TENNIS)

Guymaleman, 33.3333

- 💼 Head CEO at Unemployed
- 🎓 Schooled by a Home
- 📍 31 mules away

Wife is what I want, but will settle for friend or husband or scammer.

I am in a heavy band of metal. I play the cadmium to much booing.

In photograph, I am man in yellow.

Gwendy, π±∞

- 💼 Invented Bagels
- 🎓 Not Necessary
- 📍 12 sex miles away

Live Laugh Love. Or Else.

I am so chill. I can only hear podcasts. My spirit animal is a dead lemur.

You must be okay with my 15 craft beer children. No drinking my kids.

A PREMARITAL MARRIAGE!

BOT WEDDING ANNOUNCEMENT

Sarah Engagement and Flank Wedding announce their engagement to fuse together into one mass. Both live in Tampa Boy, FL, with their secrets. Ms. Engagement is a registered curse, working

The couple pictured after their first legal hug.

at the Hospital Made of Children and Mr. Wedding controls the clouds. The two met at the University of a Restaurant and it was love at first fight. Their parents are proud and also missing. The wedding will be held Februvember 115th, 2020-2029 at First Jewish Church. All friends and dentists are invited.

BOT OBITUARY

Brenda Tent retired from living at the age of old, surrounded by family and natural causes. A librarian from birth, Brenda was an avid collector of dust. She had a sweet heart and married her high school. She loved having hobbies and helping her sons to be  disadvantaged youths. She had no horses but thought she did. The church gave her a choir because she sang like bird and looked like bird and Brenda was a bird. She owed us so many poems.

The funeral will be held in 1977 at heaven. In lieu of flowers, send Brenda more life.

BOT STEAMY
ROMANCE NOVEL

The Plowman's Harvest Was My Own Grain

I first saw his shape, strong and man-shaped, when my car stopped having four wheels. I was on the side of the road, trying to phone the tireman to deliver me a new rubber circle, but my phone stopped having life.

"Terrible," I said to my skimpy outfit. "How will I enter the city on time for the Businesswoman Gala? I am to receive a deserved hard gold trophy."

Then the plow was seen. Sleek and long, fresh from the testosterone fields. Riding was the hunk of human lust. Straw hat on his dome, straw piece in his man mouth, straw clothing barely covering his many biceps. If this was a scarecrow, I did not want to be a crow since I would be scared. I normally wanted to be a crow.

"How-D," he said like a cowboy having his way with language. Lucky language. I wished I was words. Words of a sexable age. "Need help getting your tire erect?"

He pulled out of his grunting plow. A statue of a man. I wished I were the Museum of Chiseled Flesh so he would be in my warm lobby. But I was just the Museum of No Boyfriend, closed all days of the week.

"If you can," I lipped to him. "It is flat. I am not." My breasts heaved a hello. "What are you called?"

"The Plowman," said the plowman. He kissed the bad tire and it was now good.

"I am also a tire," I hinted, hoping to receive a sensual smooch attack. "Please fix me."

Sweat glistened off of the plowman's throbbing head of hair. Brown hair. The color of a crayon named Rough Intercourse. He gazed at me. Piercing eyes of passion. I blushed, my cheeks full of juicy blood, a vampire's snack.

"A lie," the plowman verbally thrusted. "A tire could not be so beautifully hot. May I wrap you in grain?"

"A grain girl? Myself? Currently, I am CEO of Feminism at New York Corporation. I live a life of money and gadgets."

I knew the plowman did not know what anything meant. He probably only knew three ideas: farmwork, love, and eating chickens in one fleshy bite. I wished I was a chicken, but not a crow. There's a birdly difference.

"I have a secret." The plowman flexed his brow, dislodging rich soil from grooves of ruggedness. "You are my type: female."

I swooned so devastatingly that I fainted into a lust coma. I awoke in the plowman's bed of corn. He gazed down at me.

"May I replace your clothes with nothing?" he asked, already knowing the response would be a strong affirmation of nudity.

He then took me. I took him back. Taking and more taking until there was nothing to take. We both were out of energy and out of breath and out in a public farm field.

He rolled on his burly side. "I am sorry, but we cannot be married."

"Why not?" It was my life's dream to marry him ever since twelve minutes prior.

He frowned and tears that smelled like motor oil came from his thick eyes. "I am already wed. I am the husband of the Earth. Do you know her?"

The Earth. I knew that blue and green bitch of a planet well. I lived on her wide load. I would have to get rid of her to have my man. My plowman.

I kissed his sensual cheekbone and whispered into his nose. "Do not worry, my big love guy. I will make this all work. We will be buried together in the sexiest graveyard."

I called the President of America for a nonsexual favor.

MOVIE SCRIPTS

Movie (mov·ie) *noun*: A story captured by a camera through deception and film. Only visible in a dark box with seats while consuming popped corn in a buttery bath.

Ex. *I love the* **movie** *with the character that talks words. I have seen it zero times.*

THE CHRISTMAS ON CHRISTMAS (HALLMARK CHANNEL CHRISTMAS MOVIE)

INT. SMALL TOWN SNOW GLOBE REFILLERY

We see a SINGLE MOTHER refilling snow globes with
Christmas juice. She is widow. Her husband died in
every war.

>   SINGLE MOTHER
>   I refill globes better than Jesus
>   Claus, yet still my twins are dad-
>   free. Why? They need double dad.

BUSINESS MAN enters the shop. He wears clothes
that cost money. His hands are briefcases, and he's
Hallmark hot.

>   SINGLE MOTHER (CONT'D)
>   Hi. Do your snow globes lack
>   wet? Hurry. Christmess attacks
>   soon.

Business Man has flashback to when he was Business
Boy. A Christmas tree explodes his family on purpose.
He now hates trees and Christmas and explosions. He
exits the flashback.

>   BUSINESS MAN
>   Shut your sound! I am from
>   Huge City. I bought your land and
>   am turning it into an oil resort.

>   SINGLE MOTHER
>   Rude behavior! This is a family
>   business. I sell families. I am
>   widow. My husband is now bones.

Single Mother points to her husband's bones in the
corner of the room. They are all giftwrapped in
eggnog.

                    BUSINESS MAN
All of my wives are bones! That
is America. But I must make money
for my twins to live. They are a
prince.

                    SINGLE MOTHER
I, too, own twins. Please, don't
have bought my land. Christmas is
today.

                    BUSINESS MAN
Laugh. I bought Christmas and now
it is never. Unless we go on dates.

                    SINGLE MOTHER
I cannot date because of a snow
curse. I pray Santa helps me.

Santa cannot help. She did not know but Santa was her
husband. Santa is bones. Bones help nobody.

INDIANA JONES MOVIE

INT. THE CAVE THAT WROTE THE BIBLE

We see INDIANA JONES, sweaty with dust and hatted with hat. A giant boulder follows him everywhere since it is 1930s.

> INDIANA JONES
> I must watch for boob traps.

He looks at a wall wrongly and thirty spears fire. He dodges while being ruggedly handsome. He examines a spear.

> INDIANA JONES (CONT'D)
> Being archaeology professor, I know this spear is old. From past, I bet.

On a pedestal we see the item of seeking: the Holy Crystal Skull of the alien Jesus Christ. Indiana steps to it.

> VOICE OF GERMANY
> Not so fast, Dr. Jeans.

The state of Indiana turns and sees HITLER, the Nazi's evil quarterback. Hitler aims two snakes at Indiana.

> INDIANA JONES
> Why must it be snakes? Other things exist, I believe! Like fish.

> HITLER
> Snakes are Nazis now! Get used to it. Now take skull and give to me.

> INDIANA JONES
> It belongs in a museum so people can look at it being old! Jesus was a car painter. He loved museums.

                         HITLER
              Museums are Nazis now!

Indiana hates this. He uses his whip to grab the
Crystal Skull and flings it at Hitler's German skull.
Hitler catches it with his puny mustache.

                     HITLER (CONT'D)
              Moron. Now I have the power of
              Christianity. I own Sundays.

Hitler stares into the skull. Indiana Jones shoots
Hitler. Hitler forgot to make bullets into Nazis, so
they are still his enemy and he dies.

                     INDIANA JONES
              This was all archaeology.

He tries to take the alien head, but the Nazi snakes
guard it. He gives up since he has a college class to
teach in seven minutes.

ACTION MOVIE TRAILER

EXT. HIGH OCTANE CITY

Screen is black, but we hear a piano slowly cough.

> TRAILER'S VOICE
> This summer. Revenge is a cop.

We see OFFICER REVENGE handcuffing an illegal U-turn.
He is a muscle, strong as an ox, attractive as an ox.
Might be ox.

> TRAILER'S VOICE (CONT'D)
> But crime pays. Direct deposit.

A DRUG LORD fires a cocaine gun at a baby, addicting
it to cocaine. Baby didn't want this. Baby wanted the
milk gun.

> DRUG LORD
> I am bad, but arresting me is hard.
> My wife is the Queen of Police.

Piano music is replaced with a loud hip hop guitar
rap in the key of metal. Quick scenes flash: **a
helicopter dies, a lady wears a bra, Officer Revenge
gets divorced multiple times, bullets enter kidneys,
a yacht loses a serious election.**

> TRAILER'S VOICE
> Good meets evil when Dirty Harry
> meets Dirty Sally. Nobody is clean.

Rain falls down on a funeral for all of Officer
Revenge's sexual ex-wives. Drug Lord bribed the
clouds to rain.

> OFFICER REVENGE
> I have nothing left to lose. Except
> my cool. I shall now lose my cool.

Officer Revenge fires his gun at the clouds. It is
illegal to accept rain bribes, so this is warranted.
The PRIEST frowns hard.

                         PRIEST
            You shoot the good lord, not the
            bad lord. The Drug Lord. The Me.

The Priest removes his Catholic mask. He is the Drug
Lord. Officer Revenge turns his hands into fists using
ox magic.

                    TRAILER'S VOICE
            Masks will be worn. Guns will
            be fired. IMAX will be more money.

Drug Lord and Officer Revenge both punch. Their fists
slam together causing the yacht to lose another
election.

                 TRAILER'S VOICE (CONT'D)
            This summer. A movie will bust
            your block. This movie. This
            summer.

The title is spelled with body bags pretending to be
letters: **THIS GUN FIRES MORE GUNS.**

SHREK

INT. FAIRY TALE FOREST

The green ogre, SHREK, and his ugly dog, DONKEY, walk
through trees. They are on a mission to stink up an
evil castle.

> DONKEY
> Shrek, why you so round? I thought
> ogres were strong, not chunk lords.

> SHREK
> Ogres and I are like onions. We
> make farmers money when sold.

Shrek speaks like Scotland lives in his throat.
Donkey speaks like Scotland never existed which is
more correct.

> DONKEY
> I am married to a dragon female.

> SHREK
> I am aware, but wish I was not.

The GINGERBREAD MAN, a cookie with the will to live,
runs to Shrek. He's chased by RUMPELSTILTSKIN, whose
name is unknown.

> GINGERBREAD MAN
> Help. Help me, Shrok. My murder
> would be tasty, but undesired!

The cookie hides behind Shrek's greasy, girthy
greenness.

> SHREK
> Leave the cookie. It is my friend
> for a reason. A hidden reason.

> RUMPELSTILTSKIN
> Guess my name! Let's bet! If you
> guess wrong, you owe me a baby.
> If right, I owe you a baby.

In fairy tales, babies are what you win at games.

                    DONKEY
          My babies are dragon donkeys.

                    RUMPELSTILTSKIN
          That is not my name. You've lost!

Donkey owes one of his terrible babies, due to the
law of stories.

                    SHREK
          Names are earned, not guessed.

Shrek punches Rumpelstiltskin causing him to burst
into hay, the rice for horses. Shrek kills because
this is kids movie.

                    DONKEY
          You are just like an onion.

HORROR MOVIE

EXT. HOUSE THAT WEARS HOCKEY MASK

An OLD MAN cuts the grass by stabbing it with an axe.
FOUR TEENS arrive in a car that runs on sex. They
exit car. It is Spring Break, a time for teens to
guzzle fluids and die off.

> TEEN 1
> Old man, you do not belong. We rent
> this house for week of young times.

> OLD MAN
> I am caretaker. I care. Do not stay
> in house. Kitchen is a monster.
> Witch is basement. Beds are ghosts.
> Sink hates priests. TV is a book.

> TEEN 2
> Get buried. You are a waste of age!

Teen 2 is the state jerk. His college major is Vodka
Law.

> TEEN 3
> Maybe we leave? This place
> gives me the crepes.

> TEEN 4
> Stop acting chicken. Your virginity
> is making you a bird, as usual.

The house door swings open. A little girl comes out
orphanly.

> TEEN 2
> Your sobriety is not appreciated.

Teen 2 throws a can of gin at the little girl. The
little girl turns into a TEXAS CHAINSAW, but is
still orphan.

                    TEXAS CHAINSAW
          Die, y'all. Houston Dallas.

Teen 3 makes a scream. Teen 4 makes a *Scream 2*. The
Texas Chainsaw cuts off Teen 2's body. His blood says
hi to all.

                       TEEN 1
          No! Teen 2 needs a body to drink.

Teen 3 calls 911 but a Frankenstein answers and
is upset.

                      OLD MAN
          Run into the car. Go! I end this.

Teen 1 and Teen 3 run into house. Teen 4 runs into
chainsaw.

                  OLD MAN (CONT'D)
          That is not the car.

SUPERMAN

EXT. METROPOLIS

The SUPERMAN flies on the sky. CITIZENS rudely point at him.

>   CITIZEN 1
>   It is a bird.

>   CITIZEN 2
>   It is a plane.

>   CITIZEN 3
>   Enough lies. It is a Superman.

Correctly identified, Superman may land. He is a strong white man alien. His chest is an "S" because he loves the alphabet.

>   SUPERMAN
>   I just stopped a crime. Arsonist
>   tried to burn down the river. I
>   threw them into the Sun's stomach.

We see the Sun. It is one criminal bigger than normal.

>   CITIZEN 1
>   Thank you, bird. I owe you seeds.

Citizen 1 leaves for the seed store. LEX LUTHOR, businessman whose business is killing Superman, exits a bar of gold car.

>   LEX LUTHOR
>   Oh, Supperman? Do you like this?

Lex Luthor shows he wears a suit of kryptonite, the material Superman dislikes because it kills him with pain.

>   SUPERMAN
>   Kryptonite is my kryptonite!
>   Please wear different clothing
>   today.

Lex Luthor declines to change. Superman starts to die
then remembers he is the man of steel and can talk
to steel. He persuades a steel building to fall near
Lex Luthor.

                    LEX LUTHOR
          That was building where the stock
          market lives! My money is homeless.

Lex is distracted gathering his stocks. Superman
jumps into a phone and turns into CLARK KENT,
reporter with glasses.

                    CLARK KENT
          I'm no Superman. I'm Journalismman.

Lex Luthor believes glasses. Citizen 1 returns with
bird seeds but nobody to give to. He plants them and
birds grow.

SAW 9: SAWITDABA DA BANG DA BANG DIGGY DIGGY DIGGY

INT. WHALE

A sexy woman, BECKY SEXWOMAN, is covered in blood, chained to a bed. She's in a whale, but doesn't know it yet.

> BECKY
> AH!!! Blood is supposed to be
> inside my body, not outside it!

An old TV turns on. We know it's old because it's covered in cobwebs and voted for Trump. The doll from the other movies appears on the screen, but this time he's sexier. We know he's sexier because he's covered in sexwebs.

> SEXY DOLL
> Hello, Becky. Want to play a game?

> BECKY
> Yes. Of course. Don't be silly.
> Yes. 100%. Game please.

Becky still doesn't realize she's inside a whale.

> SEXY DOLL
> Becky, you are inside a whale.

Becky now realizes she's inside a whale. She's fine with it.

> SEXY DOLL (CONT'D)
> I hid the key to this whale
> inside your pancreas.

> BECKY
> (whispers to self)
> Good thing I'm a pancreas doctor.

                    SEXY DOLL
          But since I know you're a
          pancreas doctor, I took it out of
          your pancreas and put it in one of
          your kidneys. The cool one.

                      BECKY
                 (whispers to self)
          Ah, fuck. I don't know kidneys.

A countdown starts counting down from one hour on
the TV.

                    SEXY DOLL
          Whoa, what the fuck is that?
          I didn't do that. Who did that?

The whale did that.

JOHN WICK: CHAPTER PORTOBELLO

EXT. WEAPON CITY

JOHN WICK, the retired murder man we like, looks for his dog.

> JOHN WICK
> Come here, dog. I love alive dog.

John sees BIG MOB MAN shoot his dog into afterlife.

> JOHN WICK (CONT'D)
> No! That dog was like my dead wife. Now it is dead like my dead wife.

> BIG MOB MAN
> I care not. My father is mother Russia.

> JOHN WICK
> I am retiring from being retired.

John reaches into his mouth and pulls out a pistol. 59,000 Mob Men get out of a cool car and throw bullets at John. John guns 17,000 of them in the head. They hate that.

> JOHN WICK (CONT'D)
> Foolish. You should not have brought your heads. Foolish.

A horse walks by. John grabs it and fires it like a gun.

> BIG MOB MAN
> Oh bad. He knows about horses.

John tries to reload the horse but is hit by several cars. The cars die. John lives more. He rolls near Big Mob Man.

> BIG MOB MAN (CONT'D)
> You are out of horse, Mr. Dog.

John throws the horse and it explodes killing 21,000
Mob Men. The horse lives and goes back to its job
as horse. Big Mob Man and John punch and kick until
their blood is tired.

                    BIG MOB MAN (CONT'D)
          Let's build a truce. Take present.

Big Mob Man grabs a dog from the dog store and gives
to John.

                    JOHN WICK
          Okay. I love alive dog. Bye.

John holds dog and walks home. Big Mob Man pulls gun
out of his ear and points at John's back, but John
knows all ear tricks. John turns, aims dog at Big Mob
Man, and fires.

BOT MOMMY BLOG

The Products Want Your Baby Dead

Being the Mom is never easy, and now household toxins want my toddlers to have a playdate with death! As the Mom, I like my children as alive as possible. The problem is chemicals and chemicals know this, yet still they live in our cleaning supplies and kitchen cabinets, inviting our babies to guzzle. The way I solve this is obviously through trash. If product has poison, it is now a trash resident. My little boys Jacorb and Vaxx can't enter the trash realm and the guzzling is impossible. God is a Mom. The Bible gave me that secret at SoulCycle.

But but but! It is not only bleach that wants babies gone. All these items are fat with toxins:
- Perfume
- Dr. Pepsi Soda
- Bad grades
- Most fathers
- High-waisted plants
- Babies

Search your house for these pests before your toddlers chow on death's meal prep.

Now look at picture of my boys of beauty.

Jacorb is on left, Vaxx is the right.

BOT COUNTRY LYRICS

[VERSE]
My truck drinks beer
Because Uncle Sam is my porch
I work in the field, corn in my eyes
Gimme a cowboy, as sexy as the flag
Let's teach the mud how to be a dad

[CHORUS]
I'm on the whiskey highway, driving a hat
America is my bride
Red, white, and Balloon, steak is my frat
Mail the troops a horse? I tried

[VERSE 2]
It's the pond's birthday
That catfish has a rifle, good for her
My cousin got too tall, now he's Texas
Lost my boots in my feet
God bless this mountain of meat

[CHORUS 939,493,203 MORE TIMES]

BOT PASSWORD RECOVERY QUESTIONS

Secret Question 1:

Your Answer:

Secret Question 2:

Your Answer:

-Select-

What is your mother's problem?

In what city were you killed?

How old were you when you were 12?

What was one of your last 3 asswords?

How many boyfriends is too many?

Where were you when red became a color?

If you could be any animal (living or dead) how would that happen?

Who introduced you to your spouse's boyfriend?

What is the name of the road your girlfriend made her pet?

Which model will your first car take to prom?

What city were your mothers made in?

What is the first and last name of yourself?

Which company made you their pet?

Marry your first grade teacher.

What country do you wish to visit moist?

Why did you not come to my concert?

BOT POETRY

Edgar Allan Poem - *The Raven Returns*

Ah, to be a skeleton would be wonderfully right,
My inners want out and yet I must say "Not tonight."
I write in my journal—"Buy blacker clothing."
Then, of course, without a question of being nice,
a large Raven breaks my entire door twice then thrice.

Big wings, big eyes, big beak;
Not normal bird but a Ravenous freak!
"Why be so bad?" I murmured, my voice pale with wooden fright.
The Raven spoke back, which had not happened ever or often before.
Here's the Raven's quote, "Never door!"

I thought what might it mean, as the big black bird stepped my drafty floors,
Then I recalled what a ghost had told me, "Hello, Ravens hate doors!"
A terrible fact to forget—doors filled my home as sickly Gothic girls filled my mind.
My study room was not at all safe; five hundred doors lived inside,
At each doorly portal, the Raven pecked the wood until it died.

Door after door, the Raven eviscerated with featherly ease.
"Can you stop? If yes, you will receive my best cheese."
A pause was made in the bird's belligerent bedevilment.
It stared into my soul, a red look of murder at the Raven's core.
Pecking toward me I knew I would die—for I too was a door.

Robert Frost Poem - *Taking Roads in a Snowy Time*

I'm taking your roads, yes, both.
I steal the two.
I take your woods as well, that is my oath.
Put them in my sack, I carry the growth.
I have a horse, he helps me rob you.

Oh, that is your fence I see?
It is now called mine, friend.
To acquire your objects is my glee.
Happiness is stealing outside items for free.
You want it back, perhaps I will lend.

I spoke just now a lie.
What I take, I keep forever in my home.
So it is right now that you must say bye.
Forget how you have seen me, the snowy thief guy.
A man who stole roads, shoes, mountains, and even this poem.

E.E. Cummings PoE.E.m - *the SUN isn't friendly today*

dead popsicle,
melted and now a (sticky stickly stick)
my icedinner is ruined
the SUN isn't friendly today

a fire truck onfire
the orange(?) sky orb to blame
it hates it that all days are not SUNday
the SUN isn't friendly today

{well} the Earth is an oven
a big tasty piemaker humans ruin badly
"only stars may eat the pie!" SUNofagun babbles and bubbles
the SUN isn't friendly today

"tomorrow i will be kind"
the SUN tells to me and burns my ears (sounds-of-melt)
but!
it
says
that
e
  v
   e
    r
   y
[day]

COMMERCIAL SCRIPTS

Commercial (com·mer·cial) *noun*: A series of images or noises that want your wallet to lose weight.

Ex. *I am a **commercial** fisherman because I fish for **commercials** in the sea of marketing. I can be bought.*

OLIVE GARDEN COMMERCIAL

INT. OLIVE GARDEN RESTAURANT

A group of FRIENDS laughs at a dinner table. A
WAITRESS comes to deliver what could be considered
food.

                    WAITRESS
          Pasta nachos for you.

We see the pasta nachos. They're warm and defeated.

                    FRIEND 1
          The menu is here.

                    WAITRESS
          Lasagna wings with extra Italy.

We see the lasagna wings. There's more Italy than
necessary.

                    FRIEND 2
          I shall eat Italian citizens.

                    WAITRESS
          Unlimited stick.

We see the unlimited stick. It is infinite. It is all.

                    FRIEND 3
          Leave without me. I'm home.

                    WAITRESS
          Gluten Classico. From the kitchen.

We see the Gluten Classico. We believe the waitress
that it is from the kitchen. We have no reason not to
believe.

FRIEND 4 says nothing.

                    FRIEND 1
          What is wrong, Friend 4?

Friend 4 says nothing.

                    FRIEND 2
          Friend 4, what is wrong, Friend 4?

Friend 4 smiles wide. Her mouth is full of secret
soup.

                    ANNOUNCER
                   (wet voice)
          Olive Garden. When You're Here,
          You're Here.

ARMY RECRUITMENT AD

EXT. BATTLEFIELD OF THE SAND WAR

Tanks fire patriotism in a hot foreign land while hot
domestic soldiers march with their guns aimed at
terrorism.

> WORLD WAR VOICE
> Soldiers aren't born, they're
> made when a teenager puts on big
> boots.

A helicopter fires a flag at a city that looks
unAmerican. The flag explodes and the city learns
about politics.

> WORLD WAR VOICE (CONT'D)
> Do you have what it takes to be
> in the Army? It takes guts.
> It takes going to Army.com and
> clicking JOIN button. It takes
> hating the Navy.

We see pre-soldiers at basic training. They climb
ropes, they pull ropes, they shoot at ropes. Ropes
are clearly the enemy.

> WORLD WAR VOICE (CONT'D)
> We are a band of brothers and
> our instruments hurt. All our
> songs blow up.

A woman camouflaged to look like a man uses a
computer to email a grenade to Northmost Korea.
It works so well.

> WORLD WAR VOICE (CONT'D)
> We need you. There's strength
> in numbers. Only numbers. Letters
> are bad. Do not trust any letters.

A line graph implies the letters of the alphabet
caused the Civil War. Another implies the Navy let
it happen.

> WORLD WAR VOICE (CONT'D)
> Army people are leaders.

An Army boy leads a group of soldiers into a foxhole. The hole's fox does not want them there. Too bad for the fox.

> WORLD WAR VOICE (CONT'D)
> Army people are warriors.

Holding rifles, a troop of military kicks down a house door. Inside, they kick down more insurgent doors. The doors were protecting hundreds of ropes. The enemy is doors and ropes.

> WORLD WAR VOICE (CONT'D)
> Army people are eagles of bravery.

An eagle, America's bald bird, flies into the Sun. The Sun explodes and the Navy is blamed.

Text appears: **ARMY – THE AIR FORCE OF THE GROUND – NOW HIRING.**

POLITICAL ATTACK AD

INT. RURAL TELEVISION

We see a senator, as tall as he is white, walk in slow motion.

> AMERICAN VOICE
> Bad senator alert. Supposed to help
> Idaho be upgraded to a country, but
> he has kept it a state of failure.

A map of Idaho, potato's birthland, cries. It is sadly alive.

> AMERICAN VOICE (CONT'D)
> Senator promised to mail our bugs
> to Mexico for rehab. He did not.
> He mailed them to himself. Why?
> Why?

A photo of a mosquito giving the senator a wallet is shown.

> AMERICAN VOICE (CONT'D)
> Why answered: He's inside the
> pocket of Big Insect. Pockets are
> bad to be in. Ask any coin.

Graph shows Idaho ranks deceased last in Being a Good Place.

> AMERICAN VOICE (CONT'D)
> Tax money should be spent on
> making Idaho's bridge less racist.
> Instead senator spends it on those
> bears.

The famous **SENATOR STILL BUYING BEARS FROM PLACE THAT SELLS BEARS TO SENATORS** newspaper article appears on screen.

> AMERICAN VOICE (CONT'D)
> And he spoke this about America,
> the country we pay rent to live on.

Sound of the senator's quote: "**I live in America only because I can't find the exit door. I want to live in Obama, Kenya.**"

> AMERICAN VOICE (CONT'D)
> This man is disgustful with morals.
> He voted against gay fusion and for
> the Iraq worm. He rejected the flag.

Footage shows the flag ask to date the senator. He says no.

> AMERICAN VOICE (CONT'D)
> Idaho deserves a much less
> political centaur, does it not?

The answer is unclear. Text indicates: **PAID FOR BY POTATOES.**

GEICO COMMERCIAL

INT. REGULAR OFFICE

We see a WORKER and a WORKER #2. They are computering
hard, with clicks of mouse and keyboard caresses.
Their SNOWMAN BOSS, a man of snow and status, glides
into personal space.

                    SNOWMAN BOSS
            Good working, you both. To
            celebrate, I've hired a cake.

Snowman boss holds a cake with its twigly arms.
A CONDOR flies down and eats the cake. The condor
waltzes away.

                    WORKER
            Why not fire the condor?

                    WORKER #2
            No cake is safe with condor so
            close. My cake wife cannot visit.

We see picture on desk of Worker #2. His wife is cake
woman, attractively iced. The condor screeches. It
wants the wife.

                    SNOWMAN BOSS
            I can't fire bird because I don't
            want to try. I want to dance.

The office becomes dance club. Snowman boss dances
disco. Backup dancers are camels made of money.
Office becomes office again. This happens in offices on
Casualty Friday.

                    WORKER
            What was all that for? Why do? Why?

                    WORKER #2
            It was distraction!

We see picture on desk of Worker #2. His cake wife is
not in picture. Picture is now Worker #2 and condor
with beak full of spouse. Condor screeches. The
condor's job is unclear.

                    WORKER #2 (CONT'D)
          No, not great! I must add widow
          man to my résumé. This will take
          time.

                    SNOWMAN BOSS
          Your job is to be miserable.

The GECKO enters and points its nudity at the camera.

                    GECKO
               (Australian problem)
          GEICO. A fifteen-minute phone call
          can't save your wife. Car insurance.

PERFUME COMMERCIAL

EXT. PYRAMID

We see a beautiful ACTRESS who is famous for her smell. She is on tip of pyramid, Egypt's only building.

> ACTRESS
> (accent of lusty ghost)
> Stench is deceit's kiss.

She becomes a good-smelling canoe and slides down the pyramid. This is sexified. At bottom of pyramid, she uncanoes and rebodies. Her photo is taken by a mummy, Egypt's only person.

String music plays. Music made for strings to like.

> ACTRESS (CONT'D)
> (accent of lusty ghost)
> A squirt of flower? Approved.

Actress is lifted in air by a syndicate of butterflies. This is great for her. The ground was making her smell poorly. The actress is dropped into a pool filled with Natalie Portman.

> ACTRESS (CONT'D)
> (accent of lusty ghost)
> Odor for hire. I'm scent's dentist.

The clouds notice the actress and this is bad news. It rains. It rains clocks. Clocks symbolize clocks.

Horn music plays. Strings are upset to lose their music. Horns have not earned this.

Actress climbs out of the pool using a rope of capitalism.

> ACTRESS (CONT'D)
> (accent of rusty ghost)
> Donate your car to your nose.

Now it is black and white, but with every color.
Actress walks up to gravestone. Grave reads **"ACTRESS
- YOU BE DEAD."** One water tear quits from the eye
of actress. It lands on sand. Sand transforms into
jungle land.

Trees sprout everywhere. Smells are smelled. Egypt is
ruined.

                      ACTRESS (CONT'D)
                  (accent of lusty toast)
        Your soul has a faulty aroma. Buy
        things only at Macy's, you coward.

Music stops. Horns and strings now have nothing,
together.

HOME SHOPPING NETWORK

INT. CAPITALISM

HOST 1 and HOST 2 smile, but their teeth are not for sale.

> HOST 1
> It is the hour of purchasing. What is the next product of buyability?

> HOST 2
> Finger rings for the hand in your life. Twenty-four carat golb.

We see the finger rings on a mannequin. The hosts take them from the mannequin. It can't pay for them and deserves blank fingers. The mannequin is arrested all the way to prison.

> HOST 1
> Metal circles? Does geometry know?

Geometry does not know and if told, all is lost. Don't tell.

> HOST 1 (CONT'D)
> I wear these finger rings all the time and my husband's public plane never crashes. Not a coincidence.

> HOST 2
> Coincidences aren't allowed.

The words **COINCIDENCES AREN'T ALLOWED** appear on the screen. You can buy the words for $49.99999999999999999999.

> HOST 2 (CONT'D)
> I would trade my entire citizenship to own these for one long minute.

> HOST 1
> Not required. Just pay $5 a day for every day you're alive.

                    HOST 2
          Wow, that's exactly how long I plan
          on being alive. Not a coincidence.

The words **COINCIDENCES AREN'T ALLOWED** appear
on the screen. You can now buy them on sale for
$49.99999999999998999999999.

The hosts smile. Some of their teeth are now for
sale.

                    HOST 1
          We have a phone call. Time to put
          our voices into another ear.

It's the mannequin calling from prison. It has told
geometry.

LAWYER COMMERCIAL

INT. FIRM LAW ROOM

A LAWYER stands next to a shelf with books. The books are very wide. They have eaten too many words.

> LAWYER
> Have you been hurt in an accidental car? Has the government sold your lungs without asking nicely? Are you Mesothelioma? Answer me!

The lawyer opens a briefcase. He closes it. Case closed.

> LAWYER (CONT'D)
> If so, you can act entitled for money. I'll help. I graduated from lawn school and all my teachers were bitten by dogs.

Words scroll across bottom of the screen. These are cases the lawyer takes: **UNFAIR STABBING, ILLEGAL SHOES, MUSIC TOO CANADIAN, SUE THE RAIN, DIVORCE YOUR TOILET, FAKE SONS.**

> LAWYER (CONT'D)
> I have been a lawyer for over thirty-five weekends and I'm currently dating the Bill of Rights for fun.

We see the Bill of Rights. It's in love. The lawyer will break its heart. There's nothing we can do.

> LAWYER (CONT'D)
> Let me use it to send your asbestos to court. I will wear two suits and I promise to steal the judge's gavel for you.

The lawyer opens up the jacket of his first suit. Millions of gavels pour out. His promise has worth.

                    LAWYER (CONT'D)
          My clients never go to jail town.

We see his past clients: **a tornado, a tornado, a
tornado.**

                    LAWYER (CONT'D)
          Remember, you don't pay any money
          unless you pay us money. Call for
          a free use of phone.

The phone digits appear. It's your social security
number.

INFOMERCIAL

INT. GARAGE

A man uses a saw to cut up a different saw.

> VOICEOVER
> Has this ever happened to you?

The man's saw explodes. He is unhurt, but angry.

> VOICEOVER (CONT'D)
> Your saw explodes, but doesn't
> leave a delicious plate of lasagna
> at the point of explosion?

The man looks toward the screen.

> MAN
> Life without lasagna isn't life!

A giant red X appears over the man, indicating he
should die.

> VOICEOVER
> Hashtag Never again!

CUT TO:

INT. MORE FUCKABLE GARAGE

A more fuckable man uses a saw to cut up a pile
of teeth.

> VOICEOVER
> Just watch.

The man continues to saw.

> VOICEOVER (CONT'D)
> Keep watching.

The man continues to saw.

                    VOICEOVER (CONT'D)
          Any second now.

The man's saw explodes. After the smoke clears, there
is a delicious plate of lasagna on top of the pile
of teeth.

                MORE FUCKABLE MAN
          These teeth can stay!

Whatever product that makes this happen is never
mentioned.

BOT SHAKESPEARE

MUCH ROMEO ABOUT THE TWELFTH SHREW KING

Act 1: Scene 1 - Romeo's Palace in Paris, London

Enter ROMEO holding a skull bone.

ROMEO
O, I grasp an old head!
Skin, hair, and eyes eaten by the hungry worm;
I call this hungry worm Death.
I give worms names; a noble profession for a palace-haver.
Alas, my enemy desires worms to have no names!
He is the Shrew King, the twin brother of my twin brother.
O, ha, fie, alas, forsooth!
He shall never venture into the Romeo realm.

Enter LADY MACBETH and MAN MACBETH. They know Romeo from seeing plays.

LADY MACBETH
Hark! Romeo, the Shrew King arrives on a boat of horses.

ROMEO
A malevolent harking you have harked me!
The Shrew King is boldly buxom.
Summon my fairy army.

MAN MACBETH
Your fairy army hath been slain'd by a magic witch in a boorish dream.

ROMEO
Witches are female lawyers!
Summon the Denmark ghost father.
It is day, but I'll make him my knight.
Ghosts are strong; fathers are stronger.

LADY MACBETH
Hark! The fatherly spirit cannot depart Denmark.
He is busy being a parent.

A VENICE MERCHANT enters.

VENICE MERCHANT
I have sold Venice.

Exeunt VENICE MERCHANT.

ROMEO
The smell of the Shrek King taints that sale!
Those water roads lead his crown to me.
Tell, what soldiers have I?

MAN MACBETH
Sirrah, you have me and my love.

LADY MACBETH daggers herself and is slain'd.

MAN MACBETH
Sirrah, you have me.

The SHREW KING enters covered in crowns.

SHREW KING
O, a foul stench I see with my nose!
This must be the Romeo house.
I will kill him;
Kill him for naming worms!

MAN MACBETH
No Romeo death will occur while I am not dead!

MAN MACBETH aims his fist at the SHREW KING.

SHREW KING
Your finger fist brings me no scare!
I possess a sword of murderly nature.
Have a sample, sir I have just met.

SHREW KING debloods MAN MACBETH with his sword.

MAN MACBETH
You wretch!
Now I must visit my wifely wife in Death country.
Be strong, fair Romeo;
Remember me as your friend and as a man.

MAN MACBETH is slain'd by the deblooding.

ROMEO
I will always remember you Macdeath.

SHREW KING
The time for remembering has vanished, Romeo.
The time for being killed has appeared!

SHREW KING flaps his sword at ROMEO. ROMEO throws the skull bone at SHREW KING's head.

SHREW KING
O, a head has struck my head!
My brains are scrambled and wrong.
Where be I? Who are I? What day is this?

ROMEO
'Tis Romeo Day, knave.
The day where all worms receive names and all Shrew Kings stop living.

SHREW KING
O.

ROMEO summons his worm soldiers to devour the SHREW KING.

SHREW KING
All monarchs must die in this manner.

SHREW KING is slain'd by the worms of fate.

ROMEO
A day of events and lifeless bodies.
Romeo Day inspires a thirst in my bodily humors.
A glass of wine will settle my sobriety.

ROMEO drinks a vial of poison.

ROMEO
O, wine does not transport in a vial!

Wicked, wicked trickster of destiny.
'Tis poison I poured down my tongue!
Alas, ere I die, one more name shall I entrust to a worm.

ROMEO looks at his worm soldiers and grabs the one with the least names.

ROMEO
You shall be called Worm Macbeth.

ROMEO is slain'd by poison juice.

Act 1: Scene 2 - Inside Juliet's Hair

BOT COLLEGE APPLICATION ESSAY

In the box below, please write an essay on why you would like to attend college.

I am a student with many grades. Furthermore, my curriculars are extra. Chess club, competitive French team, and varsity prom is where I am when not calculating which of my teacher's brains I will turn into my library. I am a Junior but have the bones of a Señor according to the school's spirit. I also play the ball sport. Last year we were Steak Champions and I dunked my uniform in points.

Personally, I have a statement. Furthermore, when I was seven, my grandpa died. It was sad, since I was only ten. After funeral, I remembered what grandpa told me when I was nineteen and he was not fully dead. "Go to college for four years, grandboy." Furthermore, that is what was said and those words were his. If my grandpa died, I should get to own your college. It is only fair, and I am seventeen.

In life, I have known three things:
• My GPA is 3.5.
• My grandpa died.
• Taekwondo.

Last yearbook, I was voted Most Student, and Best Tooth, and Top Likely to Have Dead Grandpa. I will take these awards to college town and share them with sexy coeds.

Furthermore,
Further More

Submit

BOT GOSSIP MAGAZINE COVER

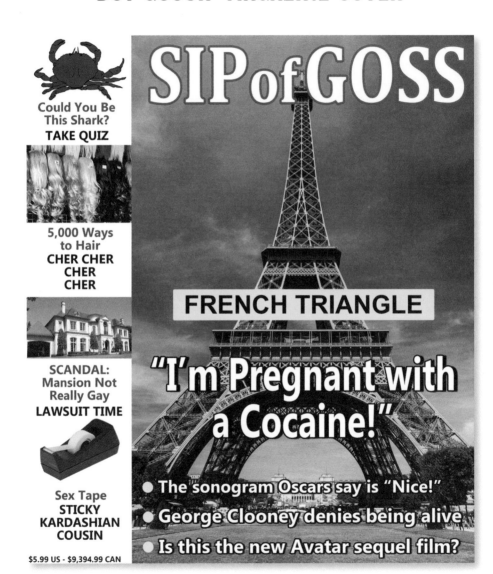

Could You Be
This Shark?
TAKE QUIZ

5,000 Ways
to Hair
**CHER CHER
CHER
CHER**

SCANDAL:
Mansion Not
Really Gay
LAWSUIT TIME

Sex Tape
**STICKY
KARDASHIAN
COUSIN**

$5.99 US - $9,394.99 CAN

SIP of GOSS

FRENCH TRIANGLE

"I'm Pregnant with a Cocaine!"

● The sonogram Oscars say is "Nice!"
● George Clooney denies being alive
● Is this the new Avatar sequel film?

BOT HOROSCOPES

Aries: *Start a new project today, like painting a painting or writing a writing or building a soul prison. Be flamboyant to get the attention of every major religion. You have the power to become the next big body of water.*

Taurus: *You are like the Earth: strong, grounded, spherical, core of iron, and named the Earth. Today, take a short trip to tomorrow on a foreign boat. Take your heart's advice: start that bird farm.*

Gemini: *Gemini, you are growing spiritually, romantically, and politically.*

Cancer: *Avoid the internet for the next few spiritual decades or you will be plagued by a plague of plagues. Invest your children into the stock market before you get too attached.*

Leo: *You are brimming with astral energy, Leo. Embrace your creative side and your artistic entrée. You are truly a star with a heavenly body, Leo DiCapricorn.*

Virgo: *You have a good five-year plan to become friends with Uranus, but bad luck may force you to retire your sexuality. Flirt with a truck, just in case.*

Libra: *The moon wants to fight you, Libra. Tell a coworker to take your place for a day so the moon injures their bones instead. Being selfish is perfectly normal when you have a celestial enemy.*

Scorpio: *Do not move to a new city this weekend. You will not know on which roads to drive your bicycle. You will ride into the lake and break the town fish, causing a riot of locals. Then nobody will want to be your emergency contact. Move on Monday.*

Sagittarius: *Now is an excellent moment to reinforce your apathy! Tinker with your electronics tonight and maybe your parents will enjoy spicy food. Avoid reading horoscopes.*

Capricorn: *Trust your intuition to sell your haircut to someone being emotional. They will thank you by spontaneously challenging you to a game of romance.*

Aquarius: *Jupiter is in Scorpio and Mars is in your bedroom. It is time to start that family you lied about on your résumé.*

Pisces: *Be bold with your breakfast. Today will be the day you decide in which decade you will die in your houseboat.*

MISCELLANEOUS SCRIPTS

Miscellaneous (mis·cel·la·neous) *noun*: Items of a variety of differences. Random matter. Can be anything except a flute. Flute is not miscellaneous. Flute is flute.

Ex. *The box said "**Miscellaneous**" so the woman who searched for a flute did not search inside.*

BATMAN

INT. TRADITIONAL BATCAVE

BATMAN stands next to his batmobile and uses his
batcomputer. He's sometimes Bruce Wayne sometimes
Batman. Alltimes orphan.

>   BATMAN
> This is now a safe city. I have
> punched a penguin into prison.

ALFRED, Batman's loyal batler, carries a tray of goth
ham.

>   ALFRED
> Eat a dinner, Mattress Wayne.

An explosion explodes. THE JOKER and TWO-FACE enter
the cave. Joker is a clown but insane. Two-Face is a
man but attorney.

>   BATMAN
> No! It is Two-Face and One-Face.
> They hate me for being a bat.

Batman throws Alfred at Two-Face. Two-Face flips
Alfred like a coin. Alfred lands heads-up which means
Two-Face goes home.

>   BATMAN (CONT'D)
> It is just you and I, the Joker.
> Bat versus clown. Moral enemies.

>   THE JOKER
> I am such a freak. Society is bad.
> You drink water, I drink anarchy.

>   BATMAN
> I drink bats just like a bat would!

Batman looks around for his parents, but they are
still dead. This makes him have anger. He fires a

batrocket. The Joker deflects it with his sick sense
of humor. A clownly power.

                    THE JOKER
          I have never followed a rule. That
          is my rule. Do you follow? I don't.

                    BATMAN
          Alfred, give birth to Robin.

Alfred begins the process since it is his job. The
Joker now has a present in his hand. He juggles it
over to Batman.

                    THE JOKER
          Happy batday, Birthman.

Batman opens the present since he's a good guy. It
contains a coupon for new parents but is expired.
This is a Joker joke.

STAND-UP COMEDY

INT. COMEDY CHUB

We see a STAND-UP standing up. They microphone so hard.

> STAND-UP
> Last yesterday, my son say he want
> to be Tony Hawk. I say, if you want
> to be bird, hollow your bones!

The audience laughs. Birds have evaded humor for too long.

> STAND-UP (CONT'D)
> This guy gets it.

Stand-Up points at a guy wearing a shirt that says: **THIS IS MY ONLY SHIRT. I USED THE REST OF MY MONEY TO HOLLOW MY BONES.** He is Shirt Man. He doesn't actually get it, but he is close.

> STAND-UP (CONT'D)
> What is deal with kids hating
> vegetables? I cook Broccoli Obama
> and my son reboots ISIS. Y'all eat?

The audience cheers. They all eat. They all belong here.

> STAND-UP (CONT'D)
> Siri is mean to me. I ask what the
> weather is wearing and she AirDrops
> my mortgage to Bill Cosby. He is
> already housed!

The audience cries with laughs. The tears go uncollected and untaxed. Stand-Up takes a drink from a bottle of cigarettes.

> STAND-UP (CONT'D)
> Lot of naked buildings nowadays.

The audience gasps. It is not allowed to bring up
this fact in public unless you are a building.

                    STAND-UP (CONT'D)
          It is okay. I am half-building.

The audience relaxes. If you are half, you are whole.

                    STAND-UP (CONT'D)
          Here is my impression of Al Gourd.

Stand-Up acts just like Al Gourd: old and white and
white. The audience claps. Shirt Man's hollow-bone
hands snap into pieces. Shirt Man cares not. Laughter
is the breast medicine.

TRUMP RALLY

INT. BIG ARBY'S IN SOUTH WYOMKLAHOMA

PRESIDENT TRUMP forces himself on a podium.

> PRESIDENT TRUMP
> I just had a phone call with the
> economy. Jobs poured out of the
> phone. Great jobs. Tall jobs. Steve
> Jobs. All at Kinko's.

The crowd cheers. It is full of real Americans (man
with hard hat, man with harder hat, gun that is
alive).

> PRESIDENT TRUMP (CONT'D)
> The United Snakes is doing so good.
> Other countries are on fire. All
> the people on fire. Hot fire too.
> Not us. Our flag is so beautiful.

President Trump salutes a flag that says: **ARBY'S FOOD
IS FINE TO EAT.** The crowd howls. They love this flag
of America.

> PRESIDENT TRUMP (CONT'D)
> I signed a bill. No more swamp.
> Swamp gone. Swamp is in Mexico
> now. It's on fire. Great deal for
> us.

The crowd chants: **FOUR MORE SWAMPS! FOUR MORE SWAMPS!**

> PRESIDENT TRUMP (CONT'D)
> Foreign powers cheat us! Canada
> steals our milk. China steals our
> milk. We only had one glass of milk
> left! Obama drank it. Not fair.

The crowd boos. They wanted that milk.

                    PRESIDENT TRUMP (CONT'D)
          But like President Ronald Rogaine,
          I will bring back the milk!

The crowd roars. They still want that milk.

                    PRESIDENT TRUMP (CONT'D)
          A wall of milk. No criminals get
          through. Democrats want criminals
          to have the milk. No way. Milk
          comes from coal. We'll dig it up.

All of the words are mispronounced. The crowd cheers.
They hate pronunciations. They love milk. They start
digging.

TED TALK

INT. PLACE WHERE YOU CAN TALK

We see a TED TALKER on a stage. They are visibly
clothed. They are shooting words from their mouth at
a crowd.

>   TED TALKER
>   My grandfather once told me a story
>   and yes, I paid him for being old.

A screen shows a bar graph. The bars for Grandfather
and Story are equal in height. The crowd nods their
hands.

>   TED TALKER (CONT'D)
>   He told me there's just enough
>   plastic in the ocean for someone
>   to marry. But we're almost out of
>   time.

A screen shows a picture of a clock that is poor
and has very little time. The crowd is angry. They
require graphs to live and this is not a graph at
all.

>   TED TALKER (CONT'D)
>   I did not believe my grandfather
>   until a mosquito made of math
>   turned me into a secret sex church.

A screen shows a line graph of all the Ted Talker's
secrets. There are six. The crowd likes the graph
since it is a graph and they like graphs for reasons
they have.

>   TED TALKER (CONT'D)
>   Now we all know exercise doesn't
>   work in Detroit.

A screen shows a video of Detroit trying to use a
treadmill but it does not work. This is a famous
video.

                    TED TALKER (CONT'D)
          But what if I told you to look
          under your seats?

The crowd tries to look under their seats, but they
don't have any. They have been standing the whole
time. Graphs don't sit so they don't either.

                    TED TALKER (CONT'D)
          Exactly my point. We need an
          app that smokes cigarettes. That's
          Economics 101 and always will be.

The plastic from the ocean breaks into the room. It
wears a wedding dress and nobody can blame it. The
crowd waits to see if this will somehow turn into a
graph.

TELEVANGELIST

INT. CHURCH BIGGER THAN HEAVEN, TEXAS

15,000 people named Christian pray until the PASTOR appears. The Pastor is twice as handsome as Jesus, the crucifix guy.

>   PASTOR
>   Happy church, sin-haters. God is
>   a calendar and He says: It is
>   Sunday.

It's always Sunday in a church. Science hates this fact.

>   PASTOR (CONT'D)
>   Let's joice and rejoice. Pent and
>   repent. Staurant and restaurant.
>   God's body is bread. His blood is
>   wine. God is always on the menu.

A screen shows the menu. Commandments are condiments: **DO NOT KILL, DO NOT JEWISH, GIVE YOUR NEIGHBOR YOUR WIFE, BE NICE TO ANGELS, BUY A BIBLE A BIBLE, VIRGINS GET NAMED MARY.**

>   PASTOR (CONT'D)
>   Confessions allow Gord to break
>   into your soul. Sing your sins.

CHRISTIANS stand and sing a karaoke of wickedness.

>   CHRISTIAN 1
>   I bought Satan a new laptop.

>   CHRISTIAN 2
>   I gave a snake great free drugs.

>   CHRISTIAN 3
>   I Poped, but I am not Pope.

These three sins are the most common. Nobody is surprised.

                         PASTOR
           The Hymn of the Hose is heard.

The Pastor sprays the sinners with a holy water hose.
Their sins are cured. If they die now, they go into
the cloud.

                     PASTOR (CONT'D)
            Today we get a special guest.
            You may know Him from being God.

The Christians are excited. God never shows up
anywhere. Body of bread, the loaf of GOD floats from
the endless ceiling.

                          GOD
                      (yeastily)
            Stop buying Satan laptops.

Science really does not like that any of this has
happened.

MUSICAL

EXT. MISERABLE CHICAGO

ALEXANDER HAMILTON, a talking cat, dances on stage.
He is an American Jersey Boy, drenched in grease and
lightning.

>   HAMILTON
>   (music voice)
>   My name is Alexander Hamilton.
>   I am the Phantom of the Oprah and
>   I never pay rent.

Every word rhymes and the music is instruments.
ANNIE, the girl with zero moms and zero dads, tap
dances to hurt the stage.

>   ANNIE
>   (with soundliness)
>   Tomorrow the sun will appear. But
>   it will not give me the parents? I
>   shall kill the sun. I get my gun.

Annie dissolves in a puff of music. Alexander Hamilton
spins around for 525,600 minutes. The BEAST, a talking
cat, drops out of beauty school onto the stage. Beast
is landlord.

>   BEAST
>   (like piano)
>   To be guest, you must pay rent!
>   Mamma Mia!

Annie, the girl with zero mammas and zero mias,
enters with her gun. She shoots the Beast with a
bullet of choreography.

>   ANNIE
>   (original cast)
>   I dreamed a dream and now I have
>   gunned a gun. Give me parents.

The Beast dies and his curse breaks. He was cursed to be in a musical. Death ends his curse. This is the Circle of Life.

                    ALEXANDER HAMILTON
                     (sung from eyes)
              I am founding father. I will find
              you father. You must buy own
              mother. I am ten-dollar man.

Hamilton searches for a father. MARY PIPPINS, a talking umbrella, flies in on her broom. She is blonde, legally.

                    MARY PIPPINS
                    (British noises)
                It is intermission.

It is not intermission. Mary's lie will have musical consequences.

PORN

INT. SEX CRATE

A WOMAN and a MAN sit at a table. The man is a tutor and the woman is a school. They are unhappy in clothes.

                    WOMAN
          Math is not horny. Numbers don't
          hump sex. Let's kill them?

                    MAN
          You are my stepsister. My
          stepsister must know fractions.

The man thrusts off his shirt and writes all of math on his chest genital. The woman learns it with her tongue.

                    WOMAN
          Oh. Moan. Moan. Moat. I am getting
          soggy with the knowledge.

                    MAN
          You are my stepsister. We moist
          stop. What if The Milf comes home?

                    WOMAN
          Milf is legend, not real.

A door opens. The MILF has come home. Is real. The Milf is half-mom, half-cougar, half-coed, half-foot. The Milf sees the math sex and her breasts scream with shock.

                    THE MILF
          No! This is legal barely! The
          trouble you are in is tight.

                    WOMAN
          This is only education!

                            THE MILF
                Yes? Then I shall help school.

                              MAN
                You are my stepmilf. But fine.

The Milf joins for a way-of-three. All clothing
on planet disappears. It is the hour of sex and
everything is hard.

                            WOMAN
                I am eighteen.

Eighteen is math. Woman has learned. Sex is the
professor.

JOE ROGAN EXPERIENCE

INT. PODCAST, INTERNET

JOE ROGAN, an experience man, talks with his GUEST, a man who has fought a zoo. Their voices might be conspiracies.

                    JOE ROGAN
          I have heard if you shoot a bow
          and arrow at the moon, chemicals
          pour out. But NASA says, "Hey, shut
          up."

                    GUEST
          I believe the gym and NASA does
          not go to the gym. My child is a
          YouTube video, full of ads.

                    JOE ROGAN
          Good points. Philosophically, how
          much money do you think you could
          kill using only my elbow?

                    GUEST
          $Thailand.

There is silence. Joe is remembering a pig he has controlled.

                    JOE ROGAN
          I attacked the Mona Lisa recently.

                    GUEST
          My dad did that for a living. Now
          there are only two jobs. Coal miner
          and Mark Zuckerberg. It's genetics.

                    JOE ROGAN
          I read in ten years, your blood
          will be wearing Under Armour, your
          hair will be owned by Elon Mosque.
          I read this on a beef jerky.

                    GUEST
         Just look at data, Joe Rogaine.
         Just look. Wow, data. Look. That's
         data. Data is always at the gym.

Joe looks at data. We see Joe look with our ears. Joe
uses MMA on the data until it is dead. The police
ignore this.

                  JOE ROGAN
                (supplements)
         We are sponsored by ropes.

MOTIVATIONAL SPEECH

INT. UNINSPIRED ROOM

An AUDIENCE sits, legs without motivation to stand. A
MOTIVATION MAN speaks with energy and sweats optimism
fluid.

> MOTIVATION MAN
> I want you to observe a picture.

The man shows an image. It is of the man, but he is
heavier, uglier, and deader. He sits in a coffin a
grave would hate.

> MOTIVATION MAN (CONT'D)
> I used to be that picture. Now look
> at myself. I'm no longer a picture!

The audience has doubt. They have been fooled by
talking pictures before, but they believe him because
it is easier.

> MOTIVATION MAN (CONT'D)
> I was overweight, overheight,
> overdosing on apathy's cereal. I
> was on the road to Depression City.

The audience is aware of that road. They live on that
road.

> MOTIVATION MAN (CONT'D)
> Then all changed. My doctor said
> I had only three seconds to live.
> That was four seconds ago.

> AUDIENCE
> Doctor time is different?

The image of the coffin man changes to one that says:
3 SECONDS DOCTOR TIME = 3 SECONDS NOT-DOCTOR TIME.

> AUDIENCE (CONT'D)
> Doctor time is not different.

                    MOTIVATION MAN
          Truly. That time on, I altered my
          life. You too can, you toucan. Take
          chances, fortune flavors the bald.
          Life is so short. Only 4 foot 9.

One AUDIENCE LADY finds the will to interrogate the
man.

                    AUDIENCE LADY
          But what if I am tired? I am
          tired.

The lady is attired in rubber tires, the dress of the
depressed.

                    MOTIVATION MAN
          Well, in Latin they have a phrase:
          Car pay DM.

The words summon a Motivation Monster. The audience
screams. They are now motivated to not be murdered.
This speech always gives motivation.

AIRLINE SAFETY VIDEO

INT. AIRPLANE

We see a FLIGHT ATTENDANT walking down the aisle.

> FLIGHT ATTENDANT
> Welcome to plane. This plane can't
> be trusted, but you can. To be
> alive, always wear your seat belt.

They hold up a belt that is not connected to a seat.

> FLIGHT ATTENDANT (CONT'D)
> There are two exits on this plane.
> This one here.

They point to their head.

> FLIGHT ATTENDANT (CONT'D)
> And this one there.

They point nowhere.

> FLIGHT ATTENDANT (CONT'D)
> If you are seated in an exit
> row, you are now the pilot.

We see an empty exit row. This plane will not take off.

> FLIGHT ATTENDANT (CONT'D)
> In case there is a disturbed cloud,
> oxygen masks will come for you.

They show an oxygen mask. It is not made of oxygen.

> FLIGHT ATTENDANT (CONT'D)
> There are just enough masks for
> most people to have enough masks.
> Now, if the water is where the
> plane chooses to go, don't worry.
> Your seat can float far away from
> you.

They smile. They are not worried. They aren't on your plane.

>FLIGHT ATTENDANT (CONT'D)
>Young children must be turned off
>or placed in airplane mode.

They hold up a child. They switch it into airplane mode.

>FLIGHT ATTENDANT (CONT'D)
>Flying is illegal.

WHITE HOUSE PRESS BRIEFING

INT. THE WHITEST HOUSE

SARAH HUCKABEE SANDERS angers her way up to the podium.

>   SARAH
>   Good afternoon. Couple of
>   announcements: I don't actually
>   wish you a good afternoon and the
>   President hates you all. Questions?

Journalists raise their hands.

>   SARAH (CONT'D)
>   There will be no answers.

Journalists still raise their hands. It's all they know.

>   SARAH (CONT'D)
>   Fine. But make the questions
>   good or I'll explode into spiders.

>   JOURNALIST 1
>   Is the President downloading
>   Russian spies into his son?

>   SARAH
>   Two things. One: If Russia is real,
>   show me it on this map, news pig.

Sarah holds up a map of Hogwarts, the wizard day camp.

>   SARAH (CONT'D)
>   You can't, because it's not real.
>   And two: The President does not
>   exist. Next question.

>   JOURNALIST 2
>   Are we still building the wall?

                    SARAH
        I will have a wall built with
        your questions and your bones.
        Every day you try to slay me. I
        get death threats. They feed me. A
        threat is a meal. I eat meals for
        meals. Three meals a day, ten times
        a day. Next.

                  JOURNALIST 3
        Why do you hold that glowing skull?

Sarah does not answer. The skull glows brighter.

BIBLE STORIES

EXT. OLIVE GARDEN OF EDEN

We see EVE, the first girlman, standing next to a smart tree. A SNAKE, the first long bug, walks on its abs to Eve.

                    SNAKE
          Eat the tree. Good tree to eat.

                    EVE
          Gord said we can't eat tree.

                    SNAKE
          Yes, but. Eat tree.

                    EVE
          Okay.

Eve eats the tree in half. Gord drops Noah's boat on Eve. Noah's boat has 2 of each: 2 cow, 2 donkey, 2 Noah, 2 3 wise men, 2 Egypt. The NOAHS unboat. Jesus dies.

                    NOAH 1
          The flood has been crucified. Amen.

                    NOAH 2
          Xmen.

                    SNAKE
          Eat boat. Good boat to eat.

MOSES slides down a mountain with a mouthful of commandments. Moses is Israel's oldest Jewish thing. Jesus dies.

                    MOSES
          Honor thy adultery, mother.

                    SNAKE
          Eat Moses. Good Moses to eat.

Noah 2 eats Moses. Noah 1 dies of hunger. Jesus dies
of Jesus. Gord rains down a plague of prostitutes.
ABRAHAM, the first ham, wakes up from 40 years of
living in every whale.

                    ABRAHAM
          Gord told me to kill son boys. Who
          here is son boy? Snake, is son boy?

                    SNAKE
          Yes, but. Eat Jesus.

Jesus comes back to life. Abraham eats Jesus. Jesus
dies. This why all carpenters die.

TRUE CRIME PODCAST

INT. EARS

HOST uses their voice to remind people they can
be murdered.

                  HOST
        On May 7rd 1983, a woman went
        missing. Missing from life. It's a
        tale of stabs, sex, and Blue Apron.

A soft song is played by a piano that leads a cult.

               HOST (CONT'D)
        The only evidence was hard mystery.

           THICK MAN MOUTH SOUNDS
        I was chef of police for the case.
        A very briefcase. There was no DNA
        in 1983. DNA is from 2015.

                  HOST
        Police were called for a routine
        wife vanish, a common symptom of
        marriage. But this wife differed.

Noise of a wife being different is knocked out of
a violin.

             OLDEN LADY VOICE
        Sarah was not usual. Tom-boy then
        prom queen then Tom-man then
        corpse. I met her at her birth.

                  HOST
        That was voice of Sarah's alleged
        mother. She bothered the police
        when she noticed Sarah evaporated.

           THICK MAN MOUTH SOUNDS
        Investigation was very police. We
        searched Sarah's house and found it
        was a house. In 1983, that was odd.

House sounds: door bell, couch slam, toaster fighting
bread.

                    HOST
          Sarah was a wife to a husband,
          Baltimore's only real doctor.

               THICK MAN MOUTH SOUNDS
          With wife crime, the husband is
          guilty nine times out of tennis.
          Weddings lead to fast funerals.

Show pauses to run a sponsored Adnan for Casper
Mistresses.

MOTIVATIONAL POSTERS

DETERMINATION

All floods start with just a single water arsonist.

PREPARATION
Always carry a backup Lincoln. No Civil Wars.

HOT AIR BALLOON

If you must be air balloon, choose to be hot.

BOT RÉSUMÉ

Krevor Last-Name

Seeking a large job in the field of work employment or else

19 Texas Avenude
Texas, TX 9493Texas
(PHONE) NUMBER
Krevor_2@Gmail_2.com

EX-PERIENCE

Wal-Mark, Pissburgh — King of Sales

JAN 2003 - FREB 3015

Put product in mouth of customers until money appeared. Voted Most Employed of 2008. Became friend with Mark.

Bus, Bus — *Bus*

SEP 1384 - MAYBE 1932

Was bus.

CorpCorpCorpCorp-Corp, Chicagoo — *VP of Interns*

AUG 1972 - UNKNOWABLE

Proliferified business dynamos into an accelerator of liquid asset client-friendly deliverables with scalability and gluten-free profit margarine. Also was bus.

SCHOOLS I HAVE LIVED IN

University of College, Online — *Majored in Hair*

1983 - 1(800)

Home School, House — *Graduate Degrease*

BIRTH - DEATH

REFERENCES OF ME

Call any human named Steve. They will verify my jobliness.

BUS

Yes, Yes — *Yes*

No.

SKILLS OF USEFULNESS

Fluent in Office Microwave.

Résumé owner.

Named Krevor.

Enough blood to hardwork for 53 years.

CERTIFICATES

Birth

Death

Gift

FELONIES

Upon Request.

LANGUAGES

English

English (UK)

English (AUS)

English (FRENCH)

BOT LIFE
HACKS

- Rub a walnut on a fractured leg to mend the bone instantaneously. Bury the walnut in your yard to impress your neighbors that you have a yard.

- Tie bright piece of yarn to the bags under your eyes so you never lose them in your crowded face airport.

- Draw a portrait of your refrigerator to show to grocery store workers. They are commanded to give free handfuls of marinara sauce to any possible Picassos.

- Always have ice cubes in your mouth. When your boss asks for a great idea, you will be able to explain you have one but cannot state it due to your ice mouth. Your job is now cool and easy.

- Burn Doritos while out camping to feed your fire. Bears will stay far away from your area, confused and afraid as to why you would be so wasteful of bold flavors.

- A bar of soap in each shoe will let you walk onto any domestic flight without a ticket or a reason. This is how pilots do it, and how you will do it, because now you're a pilot.

- A wet paper towel wrapped around your freezer will make your Wi-Fi so strong your house will become the internet. Enjoy your home's many new chat rooms. Your dog is now Google.

- Place your Christmas ornaments into egg cartons and then ask the egg farmer, "Is this what you call a good idea?" You will be offered a full refund. Do not take it.

- While being photographed, raise your chin and squint your eyes to appear more like a microwave, the appliance voted most appealing to every opposite sex.

- Use paper clips.

ABOUT THE AUTHOR

Keaton Patti is a writer and a co-median and a Keaton Patti. He was born in a year made famous by a calendar. As a pre-adult he was bitten by an overly personal computer. This delivered him the ability to force a bot to contribute to society, and is how he invented the Earth's first content. The biting computer did not attend jail despite evidence and laws. It is still at large. It should be at very small.

When he is not forcing a bot, he is on the internet searching for a way off the internet. You can follow him online if you are fast enough on websites.

This is Keaton's first literature. After learning libraries were not fictional, he knew he had to add to the silent orgy of shelved pages. He possesses much joy to put "Author of a Readable Book" on his list of accomplishment. He has threatened to write additional literatures in the future.

He currently exists in New York's City where he lives in a pigeon.

Andrews McMeel Publishing
a division of Andrews McMeel Universal
1130 Walnut Street, Kansas City, Missouri 64106

www.andrewsmcmeel.com

20 21 22 23 24 TEN 10 9 8 7 6 5 4 3 2 1

ISBN: 978-1-5248-5834-6

Library of Congress Control Number: 2020936634

Editor: Allison Adler
Art Director: Spencer Williams
Production Editor: Dave Shaw
Production Manager: Carol Coe

ATTENTION: SCHOOLS AND BUSINESSES

Andrews McMeel books are available at quantity discounts with bulk purchase for educational, business, or sales promotional use. For information, please e-mail the Andrews McMeel Publishing Special Sales Department: specialsales@amuniversal.com.